THE
PATTERN BASE

THE
PATTERN BASE

Over **550** *contemporary*
textile and surface designs

Kristi O'Meara
Edited by Audrey Victoria Keiffer

 Thames & Hudson

On the cover, front: **Kristi O'Meara/The Patternbase,** *Lava Blobs,* 2012;
back: **Dustin Williams,** *Bricks,* 2012

The Pattern Base © 2015 Kristi O'Meara
www.thepatternbase.com

First published in 2015 in paperback in the United States of America by
Thames & Hudson Inc., 500 Fifth Avenue, New York, New York 10110

thamesandhudsonusa.com

Library of Congress Catalog Card Number 2014952408

ISBN 978-0-500-29179-5

Printed and bound in China by C & C Offset Printing Co. Ltd

This book is dedicated to everyone who
has helped and supported me throughout
the duration of this project:

To all the artists who were kind
enough to let me include their designs
in this publication.

To each of our Kickstarter donors,
who helped fund this project.

To my family and friends, who offered many
forms of support during the times when
I felt overwhelmed.

And to the future designers who I hope will
be inspired by reading this publication.

I am grateful to each and every one of
you, and truly could not have put this book
together without you by my side.

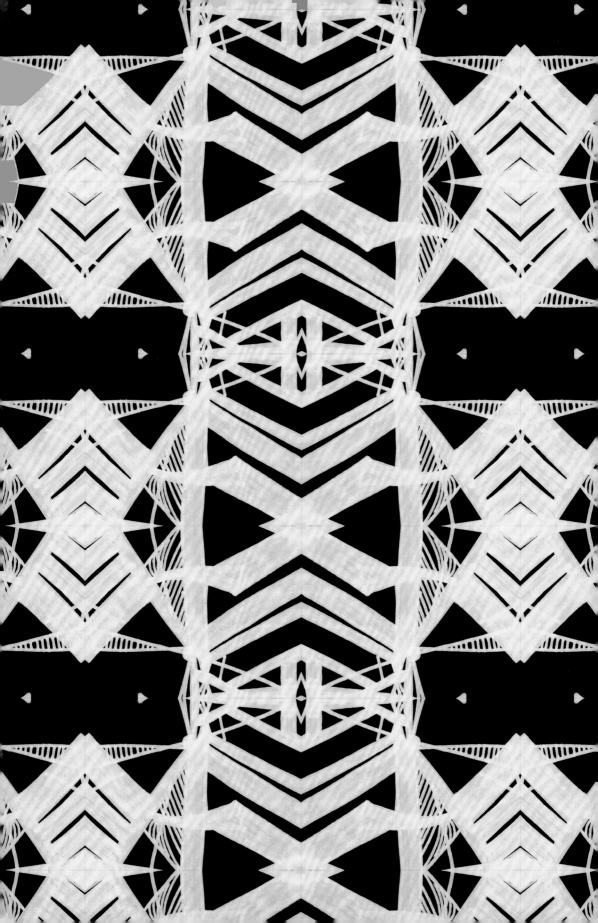

Contents //

In the world of textile and surface design, a creative digital aesthetic has emerged as a defining characteristic of the industry. Designs are more easily manipulated and far more varied than in the pre-digital age. Digitally rendered images involve contemporary motifs such as pop culture characters, collages and intentional glitches. And as a result, novel expectation emerges. Although this is exciting, many designers still value their print's ability to keep the tactile character present in handmade work and so another desirable aesthetic occurs. With the rise of digital, room for handmade approaches is still possible and can be experimented with using engaging techniques. The democratization of the industry is apparent through these new methods. Artists band together in fresh ways and it is easier for the designer to take control of their direction and designs. There are new ways to communicate, experiment and become inspired.

The Patternbase curation blends art and design to create a collection of work that offers something new to the industry. The images have been carefully chosen, and all of the featured artists are up and coming. The book is a showcase of how artists and designers envisage the future of the industry: it will challenge the viewer and designer to push for more innovation in the market. The fresh and innovative work of contemporary designers is included, spreading knowledge of their talent to a new audience and helping to open other avenues for their designs and motifs.

The Patternbase collection of designs features illustrative, abstract, geometric, floral, representational and digital designs. It also showcases knitted, woven, hand-dyed and digitally printed fabric swatches. In some patterns, illustrated images are collaged on top of each other and repeated into textural maps. In others, 2D works become intricate patterns. The patterns are thorough, detailed, layered and compositionally sound. Pattern is expanded into every avenue of expression – 2D digital renderings, apparel, installation and knit. With the future of print, pattern and apparel, the possibilities are endless and will surround us everywhere we go.

Audrey Victoria Keiffer

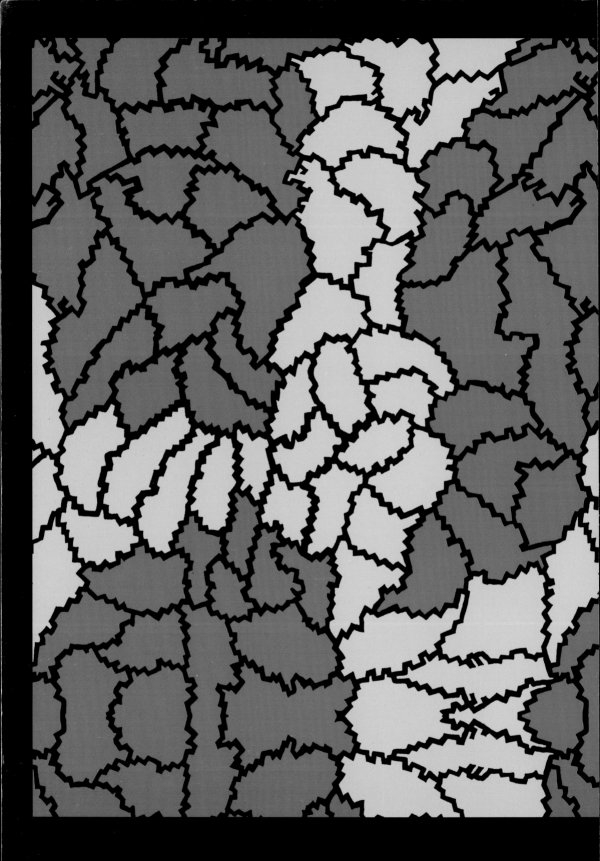

Kristi O'Meara | The Patternbase, *Fruity Fracture*, 2013

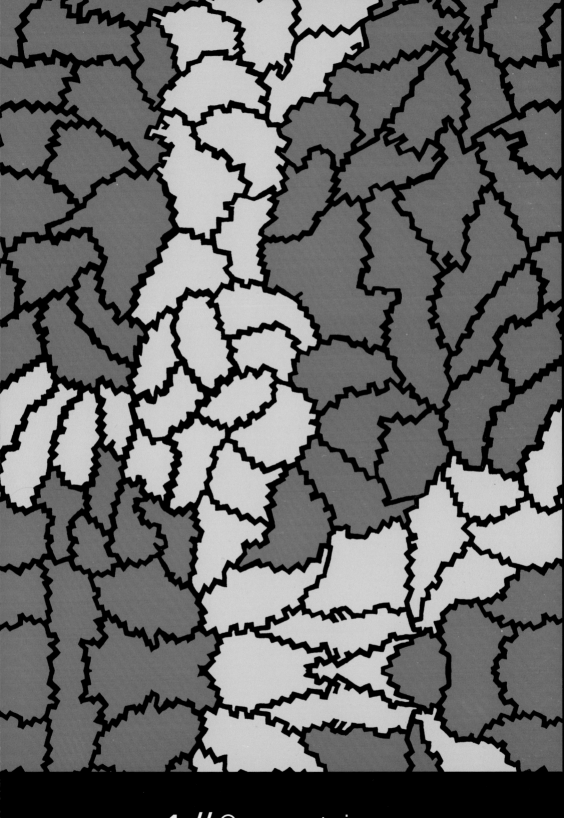

1 // Geometric

1

2

3

4

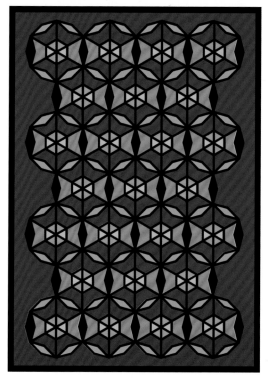

1 **Patrick Morrissey**, *Velvet*, 2012 // 2 *Midnight*, 2012 // 3 *Hypnotized*, 2012 // 4 *Adrenalin*, 2012

5 **Patrick Morrissey**, *Paradise*, 2012

6 **Anna Oguienko**, *Lunch*, 2012

7 **Jasmin Elisa Guerrero**, *Sevilla 1*, 2012

8 **Kristi O'Meara | The Patternbase**, *Powder Blue Triangles*, 2012 // 9 **Katy Clemmans | Surface Pattern Design**, *Triangle Confetti*, 2012 // 10 **Faye Brown Designs**, *Oh, the Olympics*, 2012

11 **Victoria Snape**, *Dreamy Geometric*, 2012

12 **Zoe Attwell**, *Dotty Triangles*, 2012 // 13 **Zoe Attwell**, *Triangle Tango*, 2012 // 14 **Zoe Attwell**, *Triangle Grid*, 2012 // 15 **Ciarah Coenen**, *Taurus*, 2012 // 16 **Zoe Attwell**, *Blue Triangles*, 2012

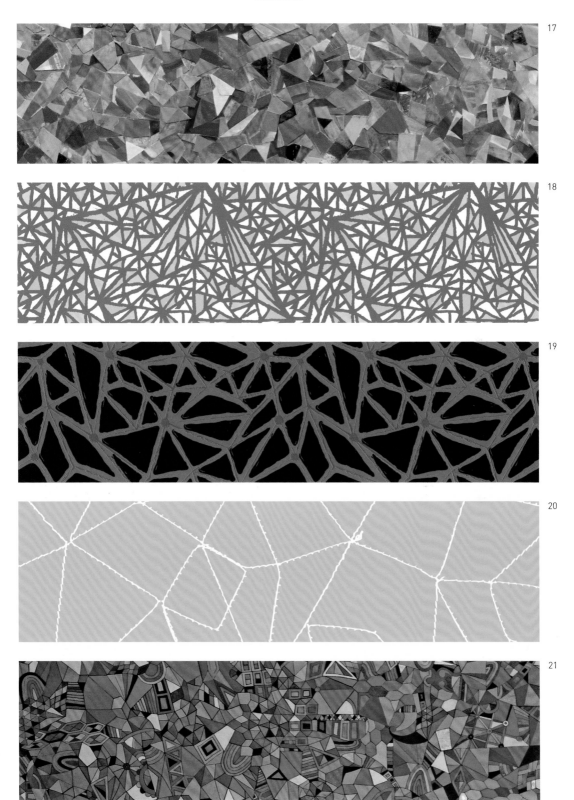

17

18

19

20

21

17 **Sam Jaffe**, *Untitled*, 2012 // 18 **Demi-Goutte**, *Mosaic*, 2012 // 19 **Schauleh Vivian Sahba | Bouclé, SF**, *Cosmos*, 2011
20 **Katy Clemmans | Surface Pattern Design**, *Cracked*, 2011 // 21 **Sam Jaffe**, *The People's Temple Choir*, 2006

22 **Dustin Williams**, *Bricks*, 2012

23

24

25

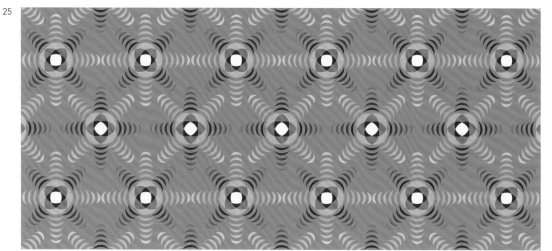

26

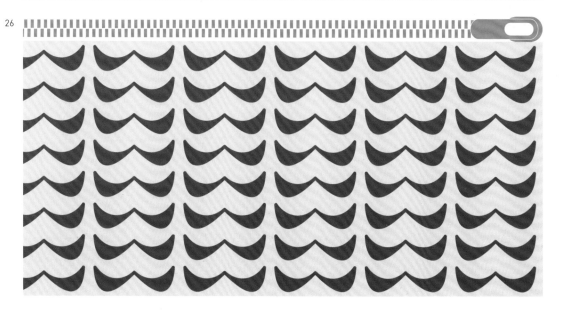

23, 24 **Veronica Galbraith**, *Good Vibrations*, 2012 // 25 **Veronica Galbraith**, *Good Vibrations*, 2011
26 **Onneke**, *Mr Moustache (Pencil Case)*, 2012

27 **Sam Jaffe**, *Self Similarity*, 2005

28

29

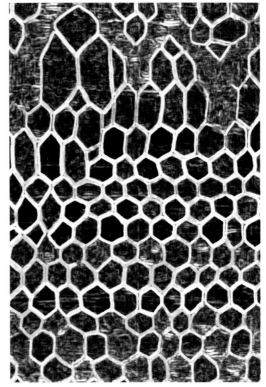

30

31

28 **Joy O. Ude**, *Make Yourself At Home*, 2011 // 29 **Kristi O'Meara | The Patternbase**, *Bejeweled*, 2013
30 **Emma Burrow Design**, *Crystalline Facets*, 2012 // 31 **Schatzi Brown by Tanya Brown**, *Dreams*, 2012

32 **Anna Oguienko**, *Logical Explanation*, 2012 // 33 **April Noga | Prillamena**, *Lala*, 2012
34 **Grace Michiko Hamann**, *Sunset Chevron*, 2012 // 35 **Joy O. Ude**, *Lip Service*, 2012

36 **Margherita Porra | Arithmetic Creative**, *Aztec Buti Pattern*, 2010 // 37 **Britt + Leigh by Brittney LeighAnn**, *Moody Malibu Mayhem*, 2012 // 38 **Kristi O'Meara | The Patternbase**, *Tribal Hazard*, 2012 // 39 **Natalie K. Davies**, *Zig Zag (In Fuchsia and Lime)*, 2011

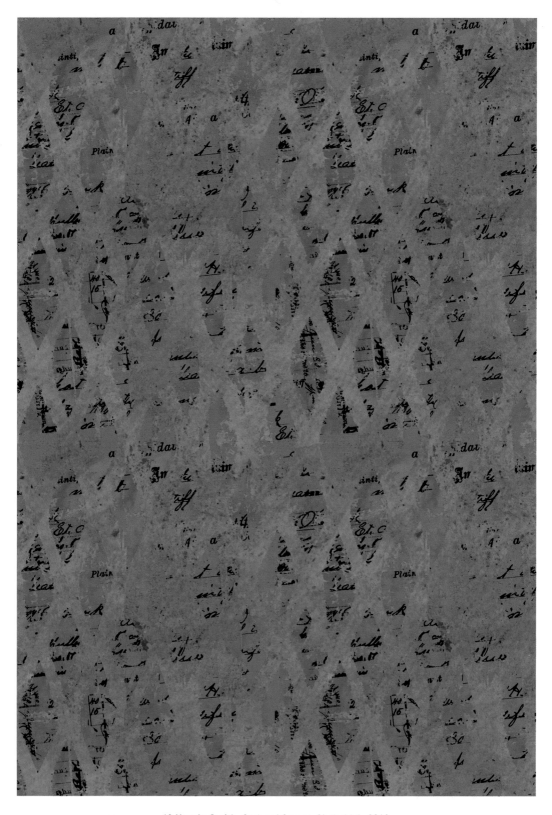

40 **Ursula Smith**, *Scripted Grunge Chain Link*, 2012

41 **Babi Brasileiro**, *Straight Tight 1 High*, 2012 // 42, 43 **Simi Gauba**, *Nayan*, 2011
44 **Elle Lehmann**, *Across*, 2012

45 **Ursula Smith**, *Teal Diamonds*, 2012

46

47

48

49

46, 47 **Jeffrey Isom | Pre Sense Form**, *Pixelation 02*, 2012
48 **Ingrid Johnson**, *Jazz Fields*, 2012 // 49 **Miranda Mol**, *Dancing Around*, 2012

50 **Veronica Galbraith**, *Bold Honeycomb*, 2012 // 51 **Natalie K. Davies**, *Zing! (In Tangerine and Turquoise)*, 2012
52 **Veronica Galbraith**, *Bold Honeycomb*, 2012

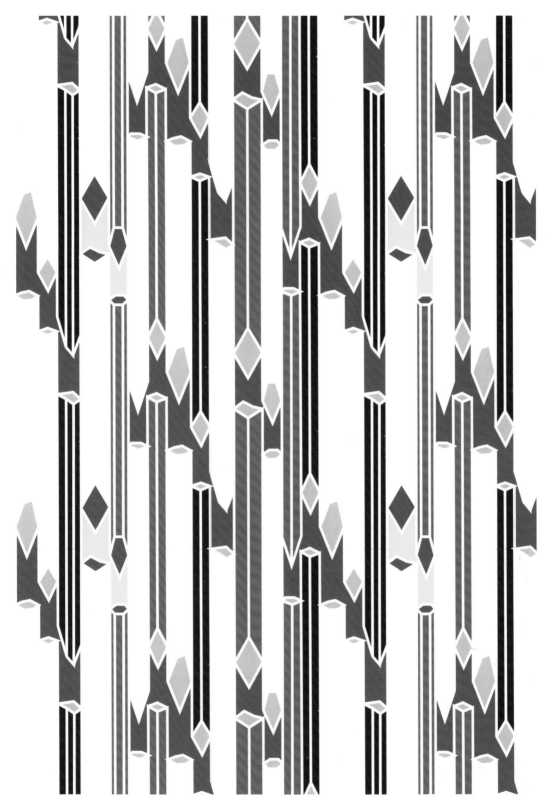

53 **Emma Burrow Design**, *Crystal Shards*, 2012

54 **Gabriela Larios**, *Semicircles*, 2012

55

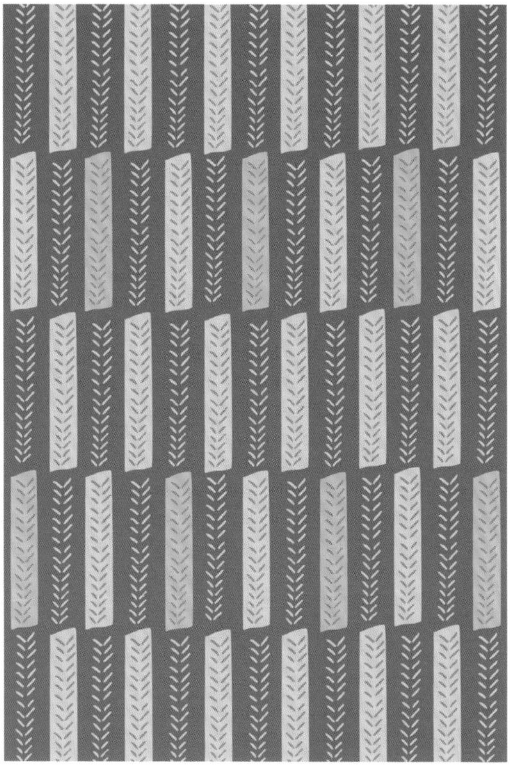

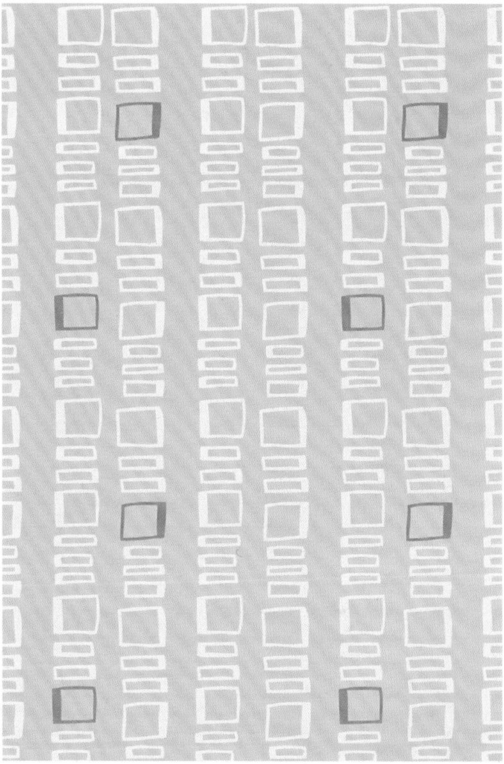

56

57

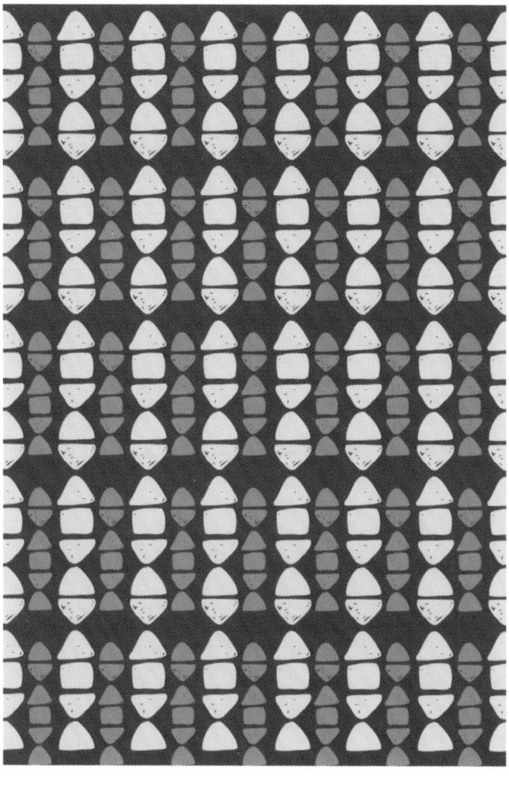

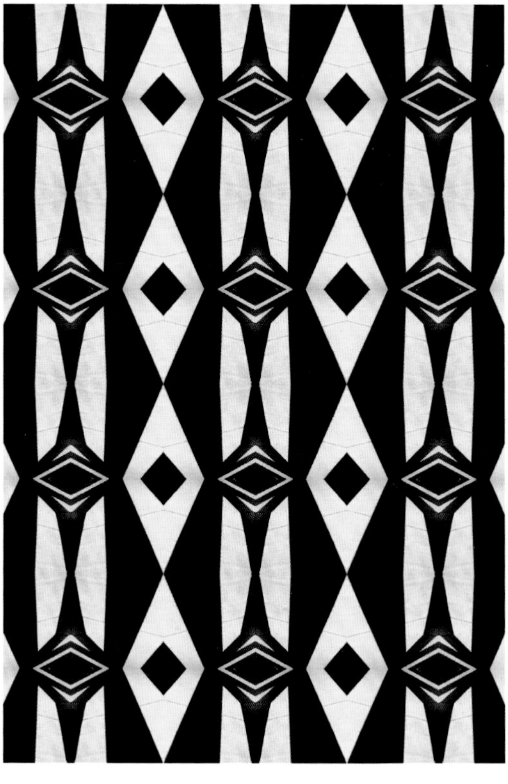

58

55 **Zoe Attwell**, *Stem Blocks*, 2012 // 56 **Zoe Attwell**, *Square Up*, 2012
57 **Zoe Attwell**, *Oranges and Lemons*, 2012 // 58 **Elle Lehmann**, *Queen of Diamonds*, 2012

59 **Kristi O'Meara | The Patternbase**, *Stripes in Seatones*, 2011

60 **Brenda Sutton | Bren Michelle Design**, *Retro Televisions – Mustard Coordinate*, 2012 // 61 **Katy Clemmans | Surface Pattern Design**, *Stitch Diagonals*, 2012 // 62 **Jaquelina Freitas**, *Brick*, 2012 // 63 **Sian Elin**, *Simple Stems*, 2012 // 64 **Ciarah Coenen**, *Fletch Stripe*, 2012

65 **Schatzi Brown by Tanya Brown**, *Geometric 01*, 2012

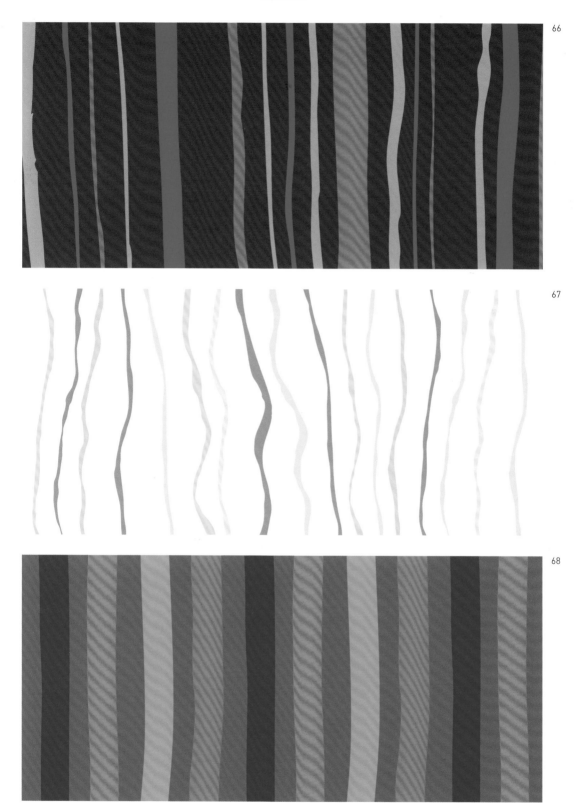

66

67

68

66 **Jacqueline Auvigne | Fine Art & Pattern**, *Hudson's New Stripe*, 2012 // 67 **Liz Smith | Elle Jane Designs**, *Torn*, 2012
68 **Veronica Galbraith**, *Eye Candy*, 2012

69 **Maraya Rodostianos | Print Paper Cloth**, *Whimsy Circles*, 2012

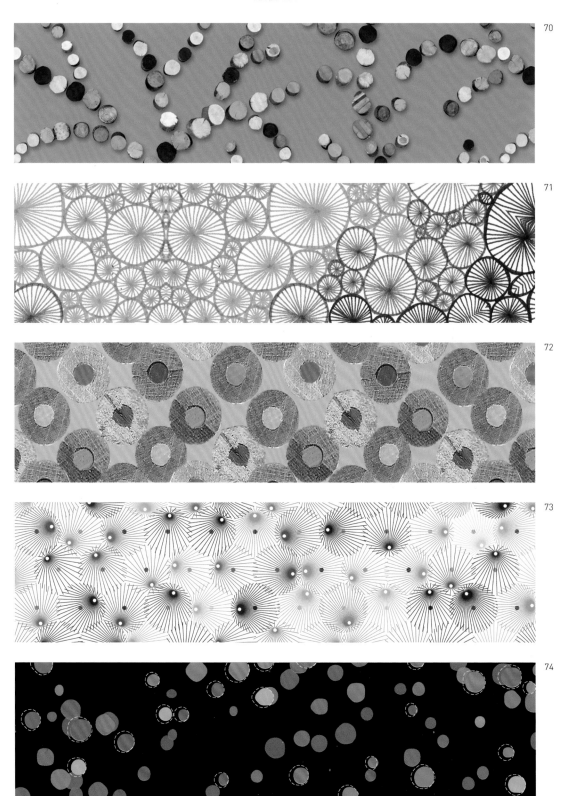

70 **Liz Weissert**, *Stick Burst*, 2011 // 71 **Grace Michiko Hamann**, *Sea Urchin*, 2011 // 72 **Liz Weissert**, *Pencil Ends*, 2010
73 **Anna Oguienko**, *Afternoon*, 2012 // 74 **Veronica Galbraith**, *Dazzling Midnight*, 2012

75 **Katherina London**, *Nitty Gritty*, 2011

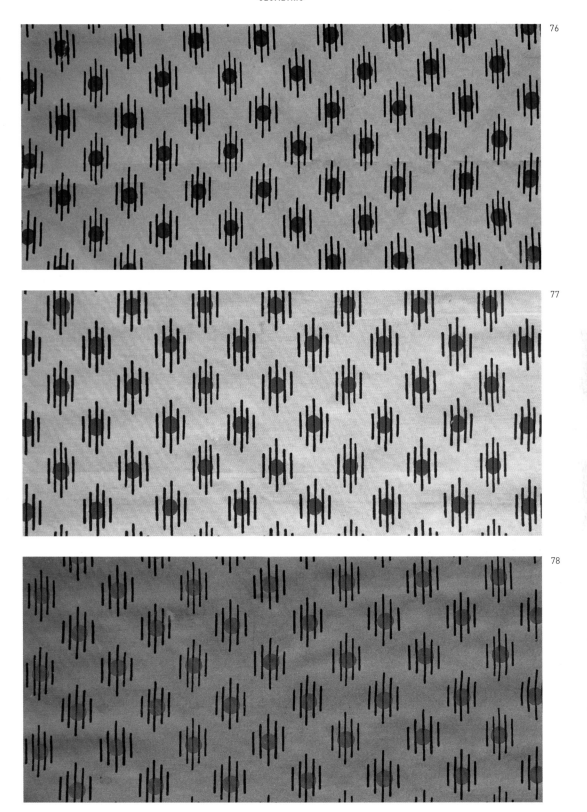

76, 77, 78 **Taylor Telyan**, *Phagwara*, 2012

79

80

81

79 **Zia Gipson | Art Isle Studios**, *UFO Pink*, 2012 // 80 **Jaquelina Freitas**, *Spiral Drop*, 2011
81 **Zia Gipson | Art Isle Studios**, *UFO Primary*, 2012

82 **Kristi O'Meara | The Patternbase**, *Quetzalcoatl's Coat*, 2011

83 **Kristi O'Meara | The Patternbase**, *Golden Knots*, 2011

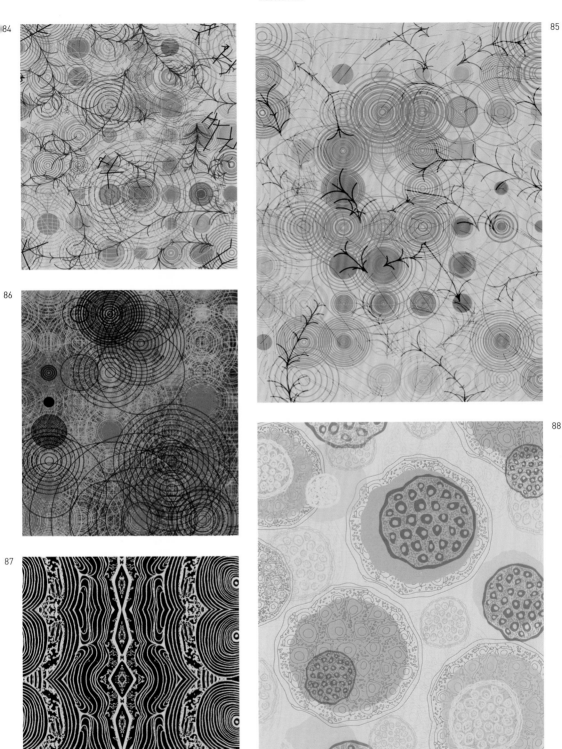

84 **Zia Gipson | Art Isle Studios**, *Circles Fresh*, 2012 // 85 **Zia Gipson | Art Isle Studios**, *Circles Tangerine*, 2012
86 **Zia Gipson | Art Isle Studios**, *Circles Firestorm*, 2012 // 87 **Kristi O'Meara | The Patternbase**, *Golden Tree Rings*, 2011
88 **Justine Aldersey-Williams**, *Lime Lotus Pods*, 2012

89 **Kristi O'Meara | The Patternbase**, *Thermal Rings*, 2013

90

91

92

90 **Sian Elin**, *Horseshoe Arch in Blue and Pink*, 2012 // 91 **Anna Oguienko**, *Brunch*, 2012
92 **Alyse Czack**, *Curtain Call*, 2012

1 **Olivia Mew**, *Morris Floral*, 2012

2

3

4

2 **Kathryn Pledger**, *Frangipani*, 2012 // 3 **Olivia Mew**, *Watercolor Floral*, 2012
4 **Olivia Mew**, *In Bloom*, 2012

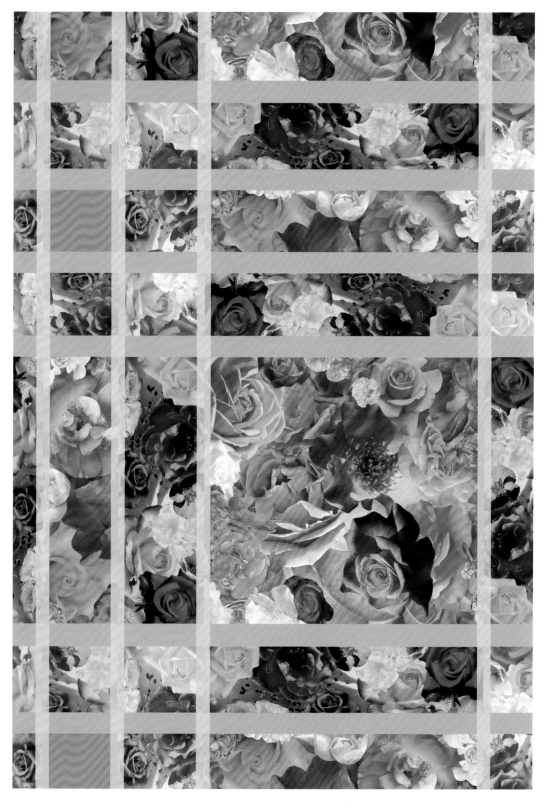

5 **Michael Earl**, *Floral Flannel Print*, 2012

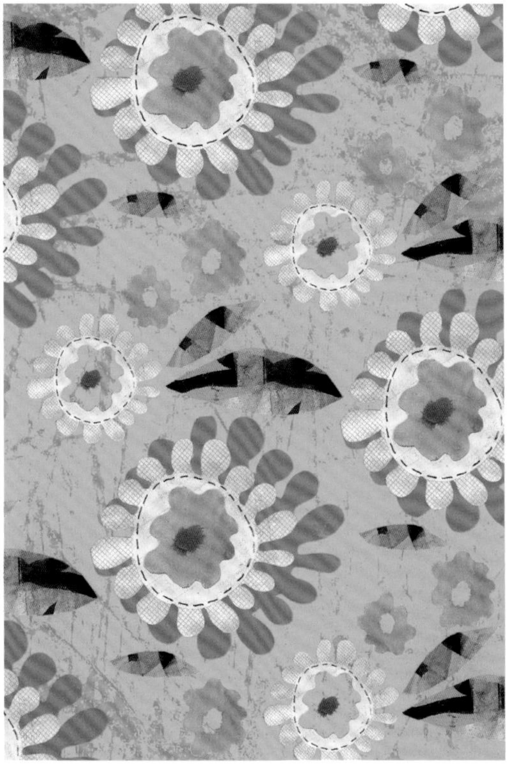

6 **Anneline Sophia**, *Dahlia Dream*, 2008 // 7 **Mel Smith Designs**, *Summer Bursts*, 2012
8 **Sarah English | Pattern State**, *Batastic*, 2012 // 9 **Claire Leggett**, *Flowerhead*, 2012

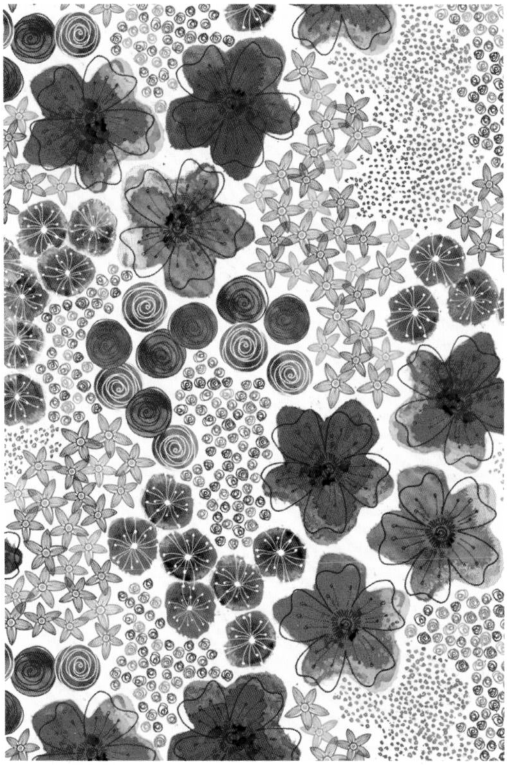

10

11

12

10 **Sandee Hjorth**, *Dusk Flowers*, 2012 // 11 **Jolene Heckman of Jolene Ink**, *Gray Graphic Flower*, 2012
12 **Rachel Gresham Design**, *Geo Flowers Blue*, 2012

13 **Femi Ford Art & Design**, *Hummingbird Glory (Vintage)*, 2011

14 **Janna Roküsek**, *Rosa* collection, Fall 2012, 2011

15

16

17

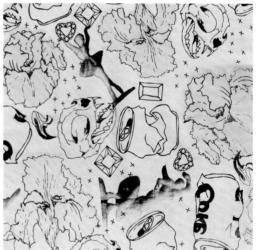

18

15 **Alyse Czack**, *Flora*, 2012 // 16 **Janna Roküsek**, *Rosa* collection, Fall 2012, 2011
17 **Janna Roküsek**, *Sloane* collection, Spring/Summer 2013, 2012 // 18 **Vanessa Hafezi**, *Pansy Stream*, 2012

19 **Kristi O'Meara | The Patternbase**, *Summer Blossoms (Ivory)*, 2011

20

21

22

20 **Victoria Snape**, *Summer Bloom*, 2012 // 21 **Sandee Hjorth**, *Sweet Magnolia*, 2012
22 **Claire Leggett**, *Lollipop Flowers*, 2012

23 **Becky Hodgson**, *Wild Leaves*, 2011

24 **Mel Smith Designs**, *Black Border Leaves*, 2012 // 25 **Janna Roküsek**, *Rosa* collection, Fall 2012, 2011
26 **Andrew William Erdrich**, *Ginko Leaf Wallpaper*, 2012 // 27 **Mel Smith Designs**, *Black Border – Trailing Flowers*, 2011

28 **Grace Michiko Hamann**, *Kiwi Bloom*, 2011 // 29 *Aqua Bloom*, 2011
30 *Periwinkle Bloom*, 2011 // 31 *Rose Scales*, 2011

32 **Katherina London**, *Wild Flowers*, 2011

33 **Naomi Hefetz**, *Tumbling Lillies*, 2012

34 **Grace Michiko Hamann**, *Anemone*, 2011 // 35 **Marta Spendowska**, *Aqua Poppies*, 2012
36 **Claire Buckley**, *Flowery Petals (Hand-drawn Print)*, 2012 // 37 **Eli Ariztegieta | RiztyDesign**, *Nested Flowers*, 2012

38 **Michelle Manolov | Pattern and Co**, *String of Leaves*, 2012

39 **Ange Yake**, *Geo Floral*, 2012 // 40 **Michelle Manolov | Pattern and Co**, *Cockle Shells*, 2012
41 **Tina Olsson | Fyllayta**, *Dark Bird*, 2012 // 42 **Tali Furman**, *Xray Bloom*, 2012 // 43 **Fiona Stoltze**, *Noguchi*, 2011

44 **Kristi O'Meara | The Patternbase**, *Autumn Leaves*, 2012

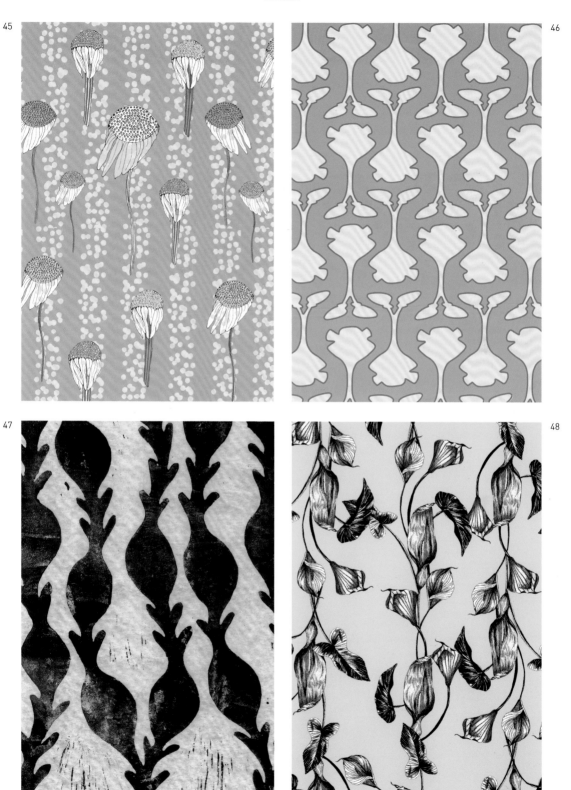

45 **Claire Brown**, *Flower Movement*, 2013 // 46 **Taylor Telyan**, *Rockin' Bod*, 2011
47 **Beckabonce**, *Seaweed*, 2012 // 48 **Naomi Hefetz**, *Climbing Lilies*, 2012

49

50

49 **Jen Gin**, *Floating World*, 2012 // 50 *Mushroom Barbie*, 2012

51 **Ingrid Johnson**, *Magic Mushrooms*, 2012

52 **Gabriela Larios**, *Yellow Trees*, 2012 // 53 **Maraya Rodostianos | Print Paper Cloth**, *Before the Rains*, 2012 // 54 **Taylor Telyan**, *Cut out*, 2012 // 55 **Marie Delisle Holmberg | Chickaprint**, *Foliage*, 2012 // 56 **Jacqueline Auvigne | Fine Art & Pattern**, *Bay Boys*, 2012

57 **Katherina London**, *Yellow Blossoms*, 2012

58 **Justine Aldersey-Williams**, *Dark Lotus Podfest*, 2012

59 **Faye Brown Designs**, *Greenwood*, 2012 // 60 **Katy Clemmans | Surface Pattern Design**, *Lily of the Valley*, 2012
61 **Marie Delisle Holmberg | Chickaprint**, *Fougere*, 2012 // 62 **Liz Weissert**, *Happy Glamper*, 2012

63 **Schatzi Brown by Tanya Brown**, *Fresh Flower*, 2012 // 64 **Lucy Hardcastle**, *Paradise Stripe*, 2012
65 **Lucy Hardcastle**, *Paradise Palms*, 2012 // 66 **Schatzi Brown by Tanya Brown**, *Flower Dance*, 2012

67 **Demi-Goutte**, *Jungle*, 2012

3 // Representational

1 **Bebel Franco**, *Passaros (Birds)*, 2012

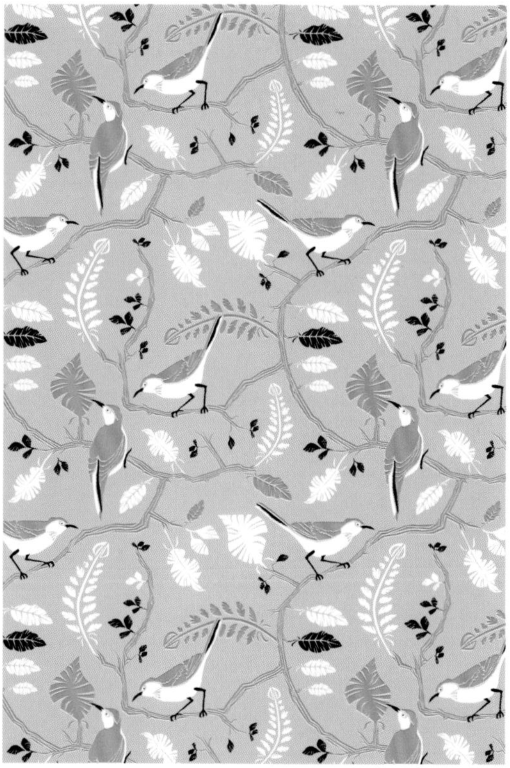

3

5

2 **Dawn Clarkson**, *Birds of a Feather*, 2011 // 3 **Bethan Janine**, *Summer Night Floral*, 2012
4 **Bebel Franco**, *Megalinda*, 2012 // 5 **Sandee Hjorth**, *Friendly Butterflies*, 2012

6 **Kaiya McCormick**, *Sparrow Jack and Gye*, 2011

7 **Lesley Merola Moya | Hunt + Gather Studio**, *Hummingbird Picnic*, 2012 // 8 **Bethan Janine**, *Secret Garden*, 2012
9 **Janna Rokůsek**, *Sloane* collection 2013, 2012 // 10 **Bebel Franco**, *Passaros e rosas (Birds and Roses)*, 2011
11 **Andrea C. Purcell**, *Sleepy Eyes*, 2012

12 **Sandee Hjorth**, *Black Swan*, 2012

13

14

15

13 **Bethan Janine**, *Pattern Birdies*, 2012 // 14 **Olivia Mew**, *Birds and Stripes*, 2012
15 **Audrey Victoria Keiffer | The Patternbase**, *Birdy*, 2012

16 **MaJoBV by Maria José Bautista V**, *Constellation Birds*, 2012

17

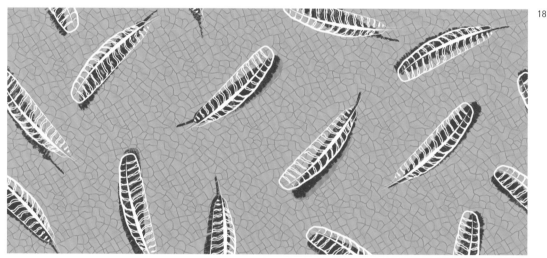

18

19

17 **Liz Smith | Elle Jane Designs**, *Linear Feather*, 2012 // 18 **Schauleh Vivian Sahba | Bouclé, SF**, *Falling Feathers*, 2012
19 **Liz Smith | Elle Jane Designs**, *Feather*, 2012

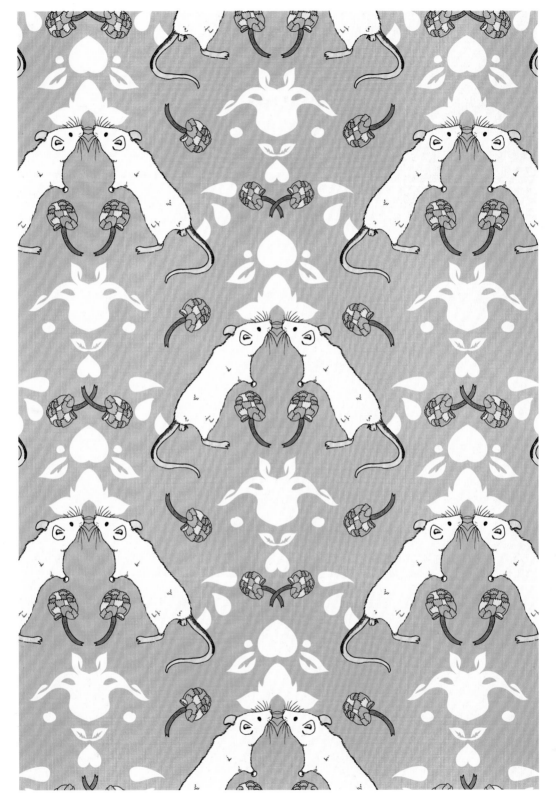

20 **Olivia Mew**, *Mouse Damask*, 2012

21

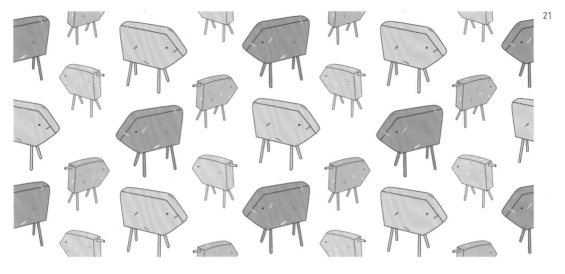

22

23

21 **Jaquelina Freitas**, *Square Sheep*, 2011 // 22 **Ciarah Coenen**, *Yearling Kitsch*, 2012
23 **Jessie Macaw | A Side Project**, *Knitted Bunnies*, 2012

24 **Katherina London**, *Giraffe Family*, 2011

25

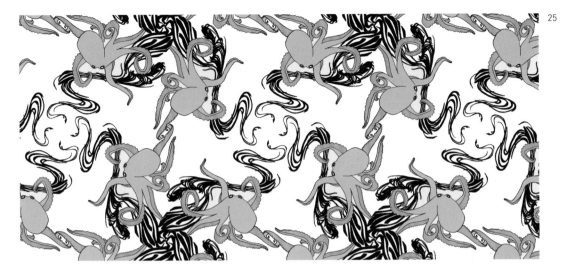

26

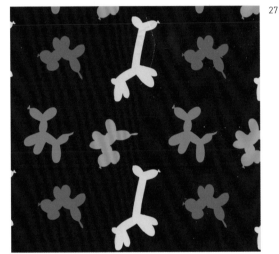

27

28

25 **Jasmin Elisa Guerrero**, *Octopi*, 2006 // 26 **Kathryn Pledger**, *Elephant Walk*, 2012
27 **Jennifer D'Eugenio**, *Balloon Animals*, 2012 // 28 **Jaquelina Freitas**, *Happy Zebra*, 2012

29 **Margherita Porra | Arithmetic Creative**, *Woodland Pattern*, 2012

30

31

32

30 **Sarah English | Pattern State**, *Rabbit Run*, 2012 // 31 **Liz Weissert**, *Spangly Mev*, 2012
32 **Jasmin Elisa Guerrero**, *Toon Toss*, 2008

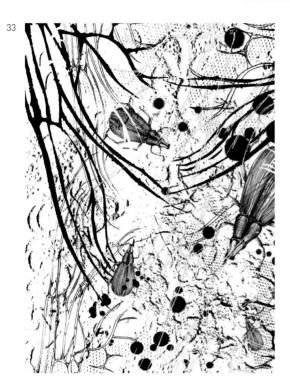

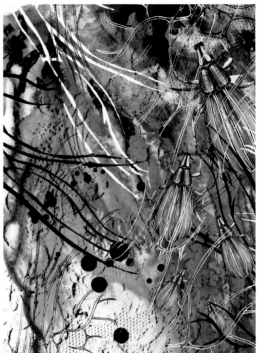

33 **Sophie Thompson**, *Pond Life White*, 2012 // 34 **Sophie Thompson**, *Pond Life*, 2012
35 **Kristi O'Meara | The Patternbase**, *Ants Attack*, 2013

36 **Kristi O'Meara | The Patternbase**, *Maggot Magnet*, 2013

37 **Beckabonce**, *Ants*, 2012

38

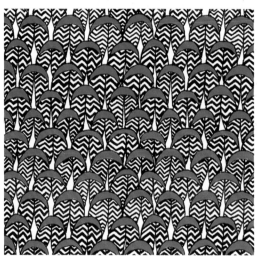

40

41

38 **Kristi O'Meara | The Patternbase**, *White Worms*, 2012 // 39 **Beckabonce**, *Snails*, 2012
40 **Kristi O'Meara | The Patternbase**, *Chevron Beetle Wings*, 2012 // 41 **Kristi O'Meara | The Patternbase**, *Worms*, 2012

42 **Kristi O'Meara | The Patternbase**, *Playful Polyphemus*, 2012

43 **Kristi O'Meara | The Patternbase**, *Mesoamerican Idols*, 2012

44 **Herbert Loureiro**, *Basophobia Pattern*, 2012

45

46

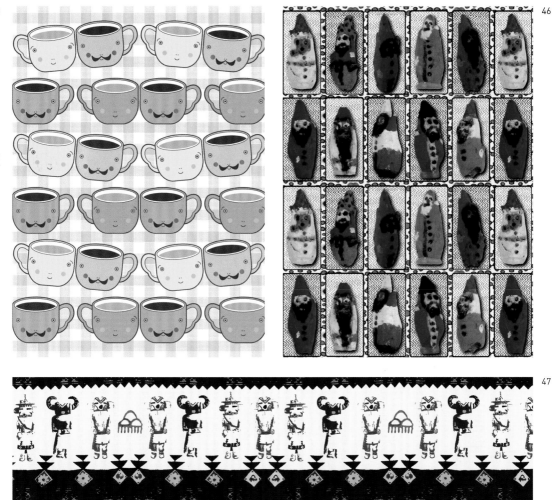

47

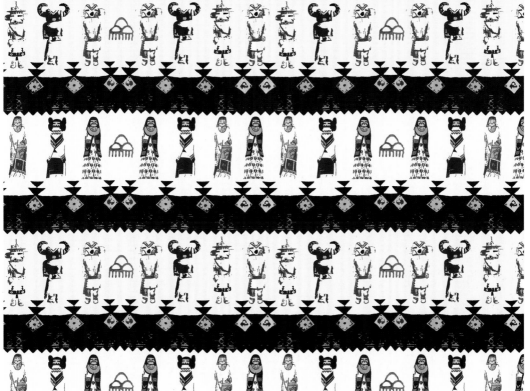

45 **Onneke**, *Mr and Mrs Teacups*, 2012 // 46 **Kristi O'Meara | The Patternbase**, *Happy Gnomes*, 2011
47 **Kristi O'Meara | The Patternbase**, *Kachina Dance*, 2011

48

49

50

51

48 **Demi-Goutte**, *Swimming Pool*, 2012 // 49 **Daniela Guarin**, *Stare*, 2011
50 **Sarah Wothers**, *Einstein in Full Bloom*, 2009 // 51 **Bebel Franco**, *Chinezinhas (China Girls)*, 2011

52 **Andrea C. Purcell**, *The Written Word*, 2012

53 **Kelly Parsell**, *Rupture*, 2012

54

55

56

57

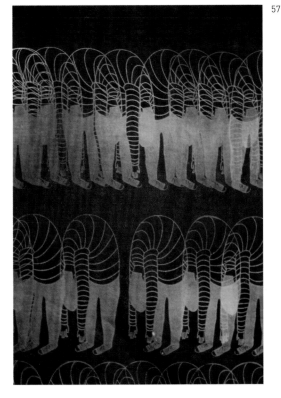

54 **Olivia Mew**, *Girl Gang*, 2012 // 55 **Kaiya McCormick**, *Jack and Gye*, 2011
56 **Jasmin Elisa Guerrero**, *Redheads*, 2007 // 57 **Young Cho**, *Fade*, 2012

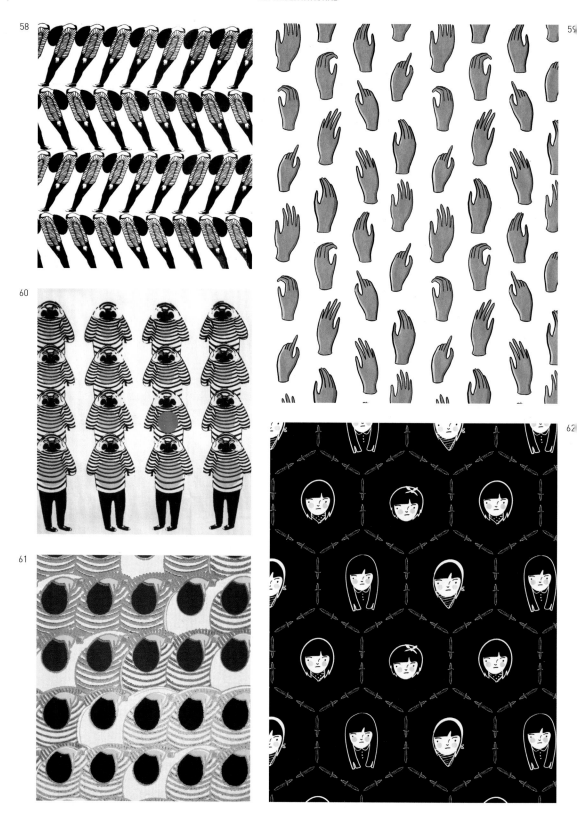

58 **Young Cho**, *Naval Gazing in Formation*, 2012 // 59 **Olivia Mew**, *Hands*, 2012 // 60 **Young Cho**, *Focal Point*, 2012
61 **Young Cho**, *Assigned Seating for Compulsories*, 2012 // 62 **Olivia Mew**, *Sad Girls for Life*, 2012

63 **Andrew William Erdrich**, *Cool Dudes: Tapestry 1*, 2012

64 **Charlotte Mason for Paperchase**, *By the Sea*, 2012

65 **Clare Vickery**, *City Night*, 2012 // 66 **Kristi O'Meara | The Patternbase**, *Homestead*, 2011
67 **Clare Vickery**, *Tent Village*, 2012 // 68 **Andrea C. Purcell**, *Mount Victoria*, 2011

69 **Jen Gin**, *Netting*, 2012 // 70 **Jen Gin**, *Chain*, 2012 // 71 **Beckabonce**, *Blue Rope*, 2012
72 **Femi Ford Art & Design**, *Tribal Rope*, 2012 // 73 **Kristi O'Meara | The Patternbase**, *Tentacle Mosaic*, 2012

74 **Beckabonce**, *Mussels*, 2012

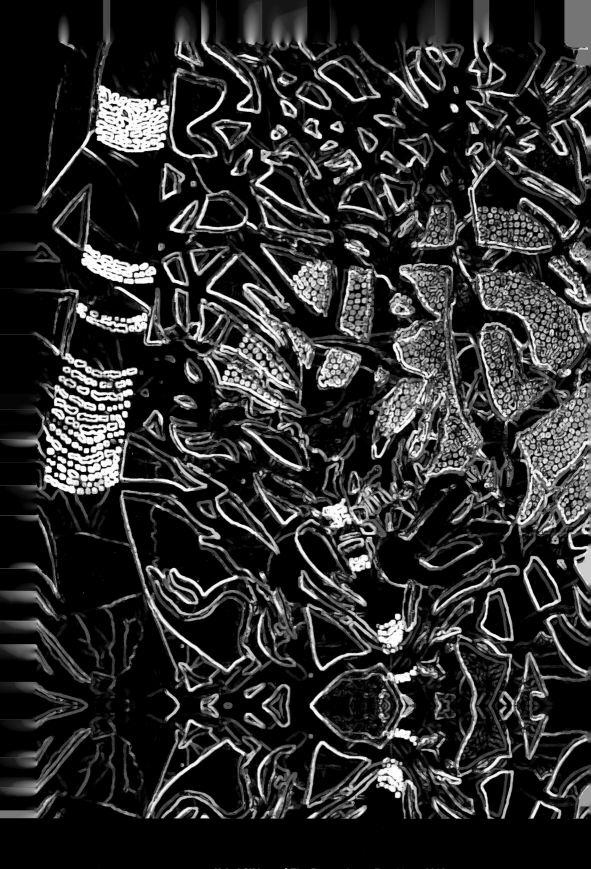

Kristi O'Meara | The Patternbase *Tree Lines* 2013

1 **H. Scott Roth**, *Untitled #4 (The New Alchemy)*, 2012

2 **H. Scott Roth**, *Untitled #3 (The New Alchemy)*, 2012 // 3 *Untitled #2 (The New Alchemy)*, 2012
4 *Untitled #1 (The New Alchemy)*, 2012 // 5 *Untitled #5 (The New Alchemy)*, 2012

6 **Patrick Morrissey**, *Toki*, 2012

7

8

9

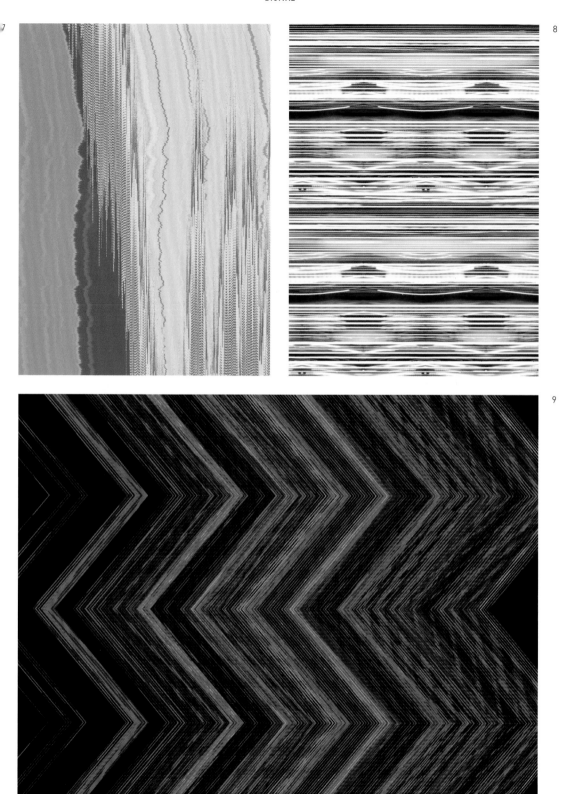

7 **Patrick Morrissey**, *Transmission*, 2012 // 8 **Lucy Hardcastle**, *Transition 1*, 2012
9 **Patrick Morrissey**, *Momentum*, 2012

10 **Emma Cope**, *Fuzz*, 2012

11 **Jeffrey Isom | Pre Sense Form**, *Anvil*, 2012 // 12 *Diamond*, 2012
13 *Grass Pile*, 2012 // 14 *Fire*, 2010

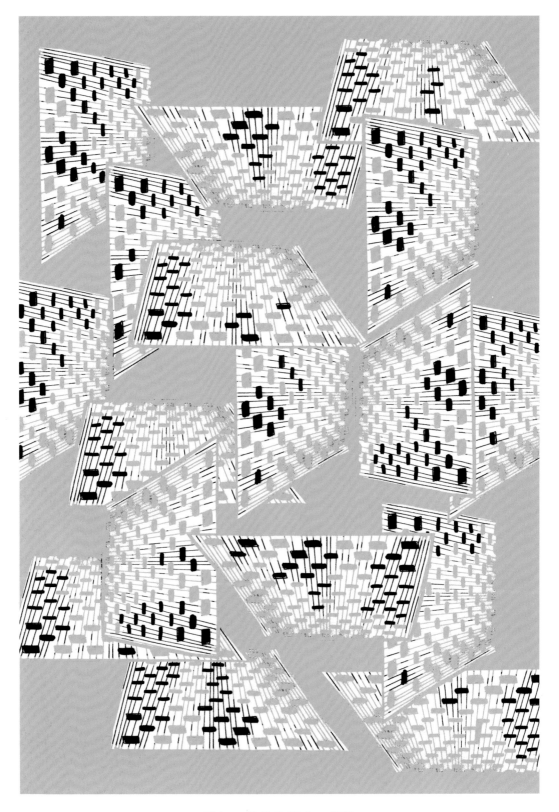

15 **Casey Mollett**, *Windows*, 2012

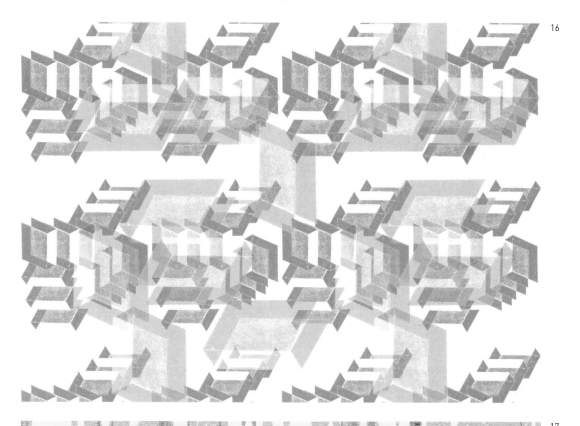

16

17

16 **Casey Mollett**, *Levels*, 2012 // 17 **Patrick Morrissey**, *Isolation*, 2012

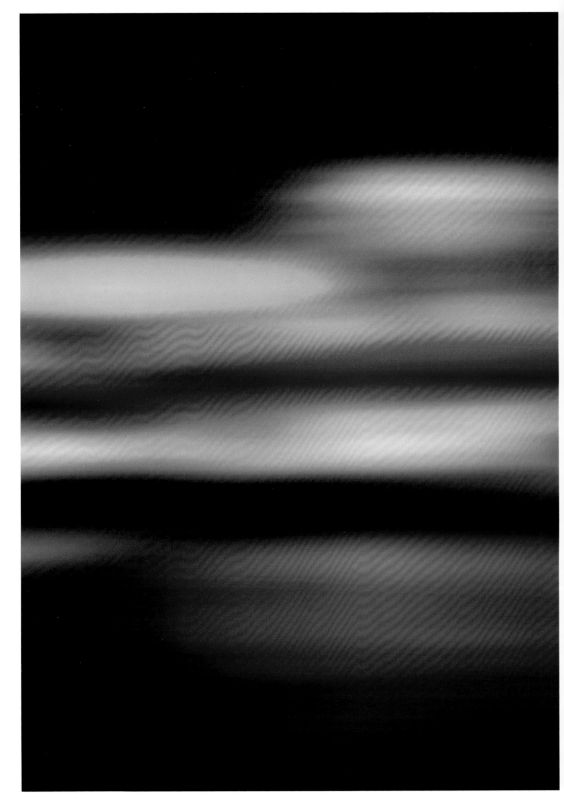

18 **Lucy Hardcastle**, *Transition 2*, 2012

19

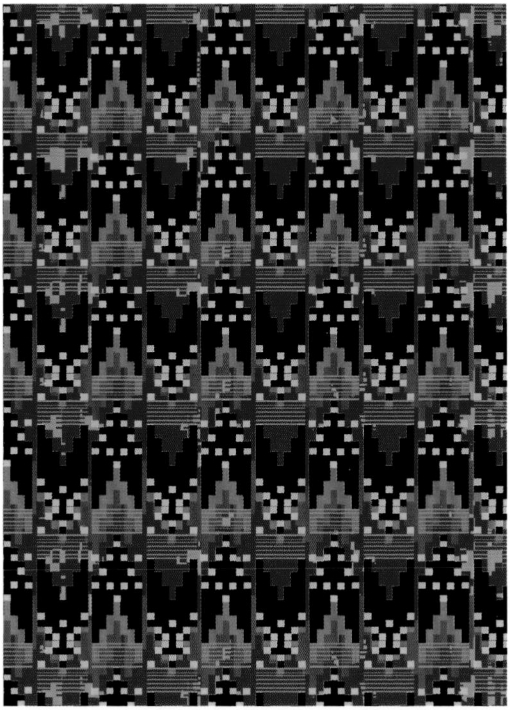

20

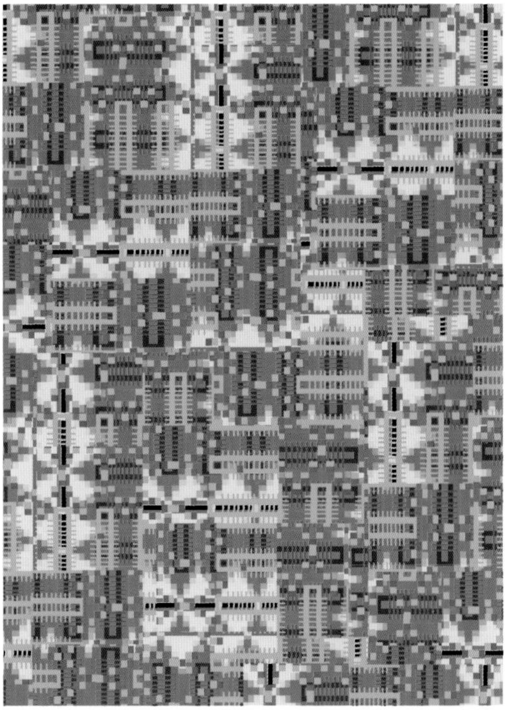

21

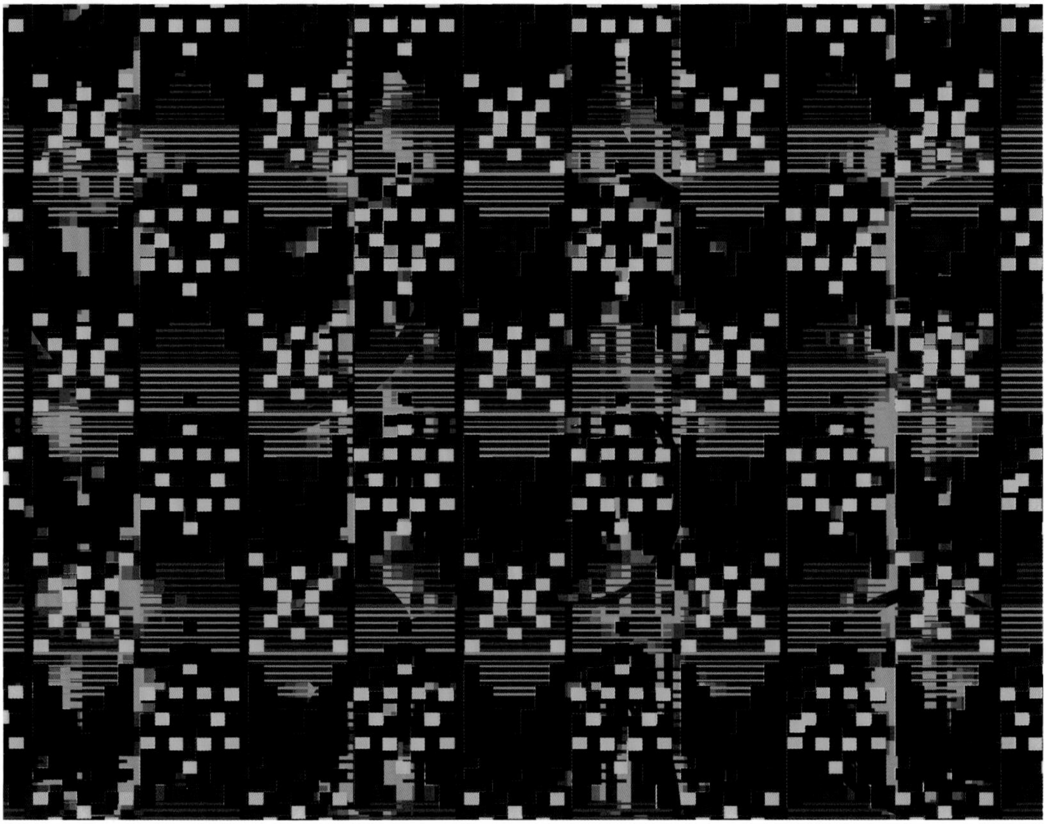

19 **Tina Olsson | Fyllayta**, *Blue Light*, 2012 // 20 *Weaver*, 2012 // 21 *Nightwatch*, 2012

22 **Casey Mollett**, *Cube Graphic*, 2012

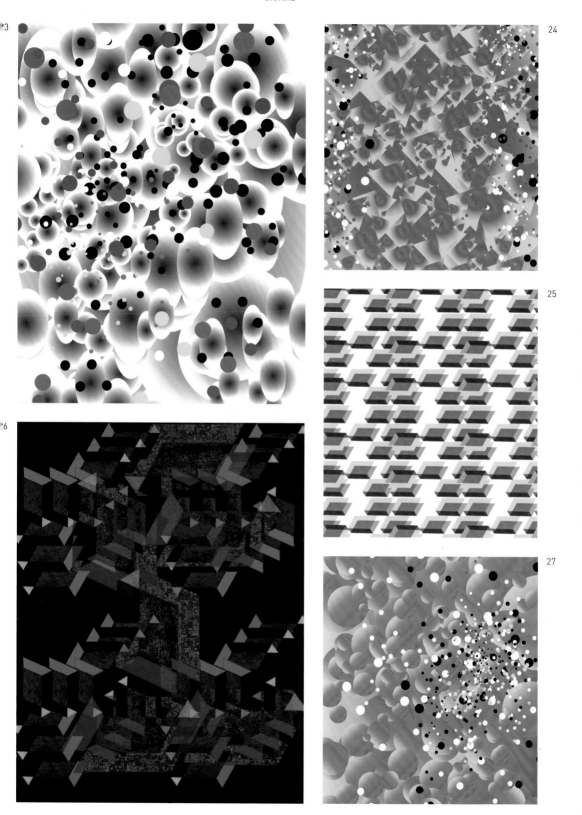

23 **Isabel Lucena**, *Expostatic 03*, 2012 // 24 **Isabel Lucena**, *Expostatic 01*, 2012 // 25 **Casey Mollett**, *Acetate Graphic*, 2012
26 **Casey Mollett**, *Digital Levels*, 2012 // 27 **Isabel Lucena**, *Expostatic 04*, 2012

28 **Lucy Hardcastle**, *Paradise Iris*, 2012

29

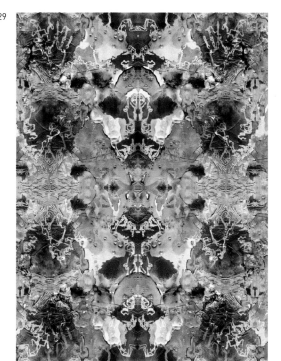

30

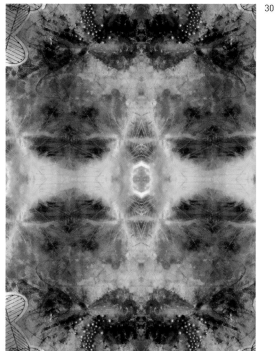

31

29 **Lauren Elizabeth Krischer**, *Polarity 2*, 2012 // 30 *Polarity 1*, 2012 // 31 *Polarity 3*, 2012

32

33

32 **Jelena Dimitrijevic**, *Cheerful Peacock Dress 1*, 2012 // 33 *Cheerful Peacock Dress 2*, 2012

34 **Lauren Elizabeth Krischer**, *Polarity 4*, 2012

35 **Roshannah Bagley**, *Basillica (Placement)*, 2010

36

37

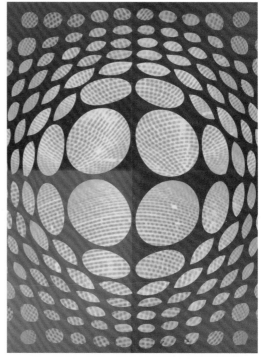

38

36 **Sarah Wothers**, *Shells and Bling*, 2012 // 37 **Joy O. Ude**, *Disco Vasarely*, 2012 // 38 **Elle Lehmann**, *Mechanize*, 2012

39 **Roshannah Bagley**, *Vintage Daisy*, 2009

0

41

42

3

44

40 **Roshannah Bagley**, *Glory Facade (Repeat)*, 2012 // 41 *Modern Painters (Repeat)*, 2010
42 *Basillica (Repeat)*, 2010 // 43 *Glory Facade (Placement)*, 2010 // 44 *Modern Painters (Placement)*, 2010

45

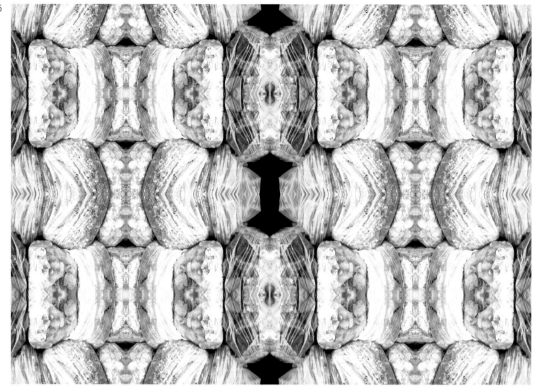

46

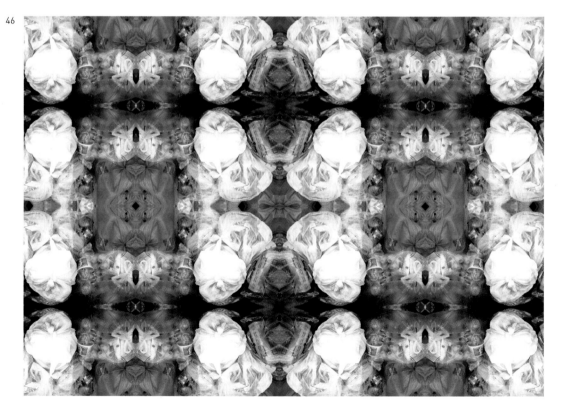

45, 46 **Ian Addison Hall**, *All that Trash Goes Somewhere*, 2010

47

48

47, 48 **Ian Addison Hall**, *All that Trash Goes Somewhere*, 2010

49 **Natasha Bugg**, *Bodycode 04*, 2012

50

51

52

53

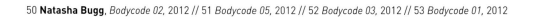

50 **Natasha Bugg**, *Bodycode 02*, 2012 // 51 *Bodycode 05*, 2012 // 52 *Bodycode 03*, 2012 // 53 *Bodycode 01*, 2012

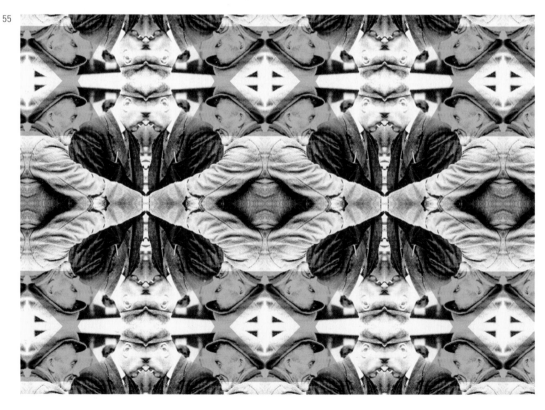

54 **Eli Ariztegieta | RiztyDesign**, *Il Giardino*, 2012
55 **Claire Buckley**, *Like Father Like Son Vintage Pattern*, 2012

56 **Claire Buckley**, *Market Stall (Photo Vintage Print)*, 2012
57 *Turkey for Sale (Photo Vintage Print)*, 2012

58 **Sarah Wothers**, *Found Fancies*, 2012

59

60

61

59 **Kristi O'Meara | The Patternbase**, *White Fabric Flowers Collage*, 2012 // 60 **Liz Weissert**, *Green Acres*, 2012
61 **Michael Earl**, *Georgia O'Keeffe Shells*, 2012

62

63

62 **Sarah Wothers**, *Dusty Floral*, 2012 // 63 **Kristi O'Meara | The Patternbase**, *Fabric Blossoms*, 2012

64 **Sam Jaffe**, *The Kelly Affair*, 2007

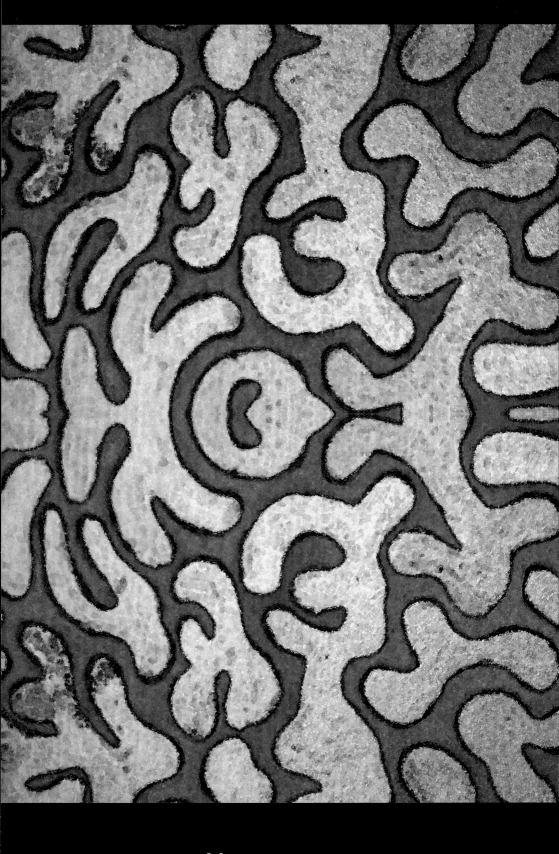

5 // Abstract

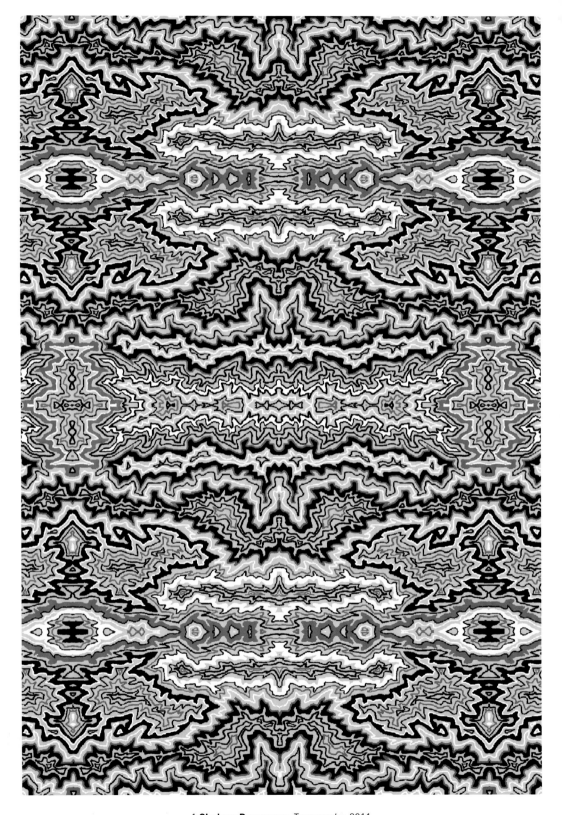

1 **Chelsea Densmore**, *Topography*, 2011

2 **Isabel Lucena**, *Ink Pattern 1*, 2012 // 3 *Ink Pattern 4*, 2012 // 4 *Ink Pattern 3*, 2012 // 5 *Ink Pattern 2*, 2012

6 **Maraya Rodostianos | Print Paper Cloth**, *Samasati*, 2012

7

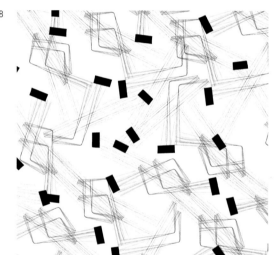

8

9

10

7 **Kristi O'Meara | The Patternbase**, *Bone + Jade Maze*, 2011 // 8 **Babi Brasileiro**, *Desfios, Straight Collection #2*, 2010
9 **Margherita Porra | Arithmetic Creative**, *Navajo Patchwork Pattern*, 2012 // 10 **Kristi O'Meara | The Patternbase**,
Lava Blobs, 2012

11 **Kristi O'Meara | The Patternbase**, *Cardboard Tunnels*, 2012

12

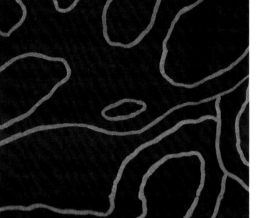

13

14

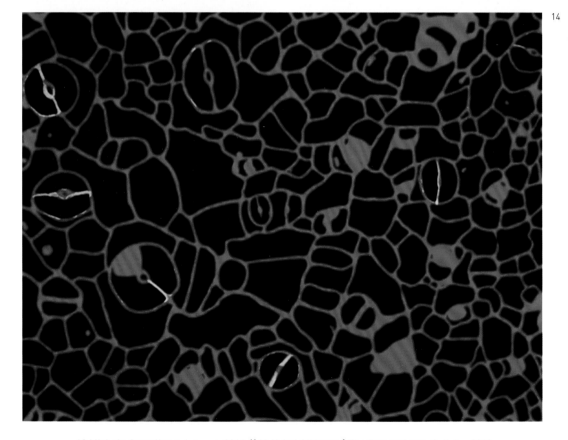

12 **Michele Castellano**, *Igneous*, 2011 // 13 **Kristi O'Meara | The Patternbase**, *Cellular*, 2012
14 **Michele Castellano**, *Micro*, 2010

15 **Michael Earl**, *Quarries*, 2012

16

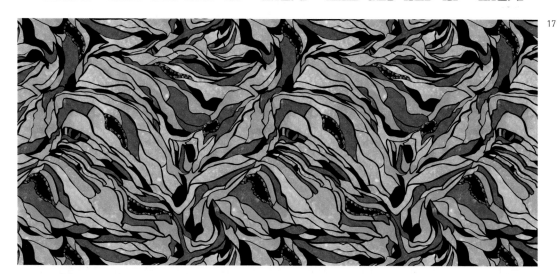

17

18

16 **Ingrid Johnson**, *Rice Galaxy*, 2012 // 17 *Rice Galaxy Black*, 2012
18 **Ange Yake**, *Shards*, 2011

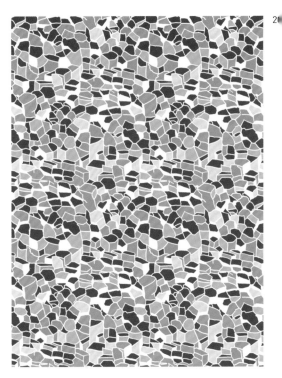

19 **Clare Vickery**, *Mountain Cyclists*, 2012 // 20 **Emma Burrow Design**, *Basalt Steps*, 2012
21 **Lynnette Miranda**, *Untitled (Rocks)*, 2012

22 **Emma Formstone**, *Agates*, 2012

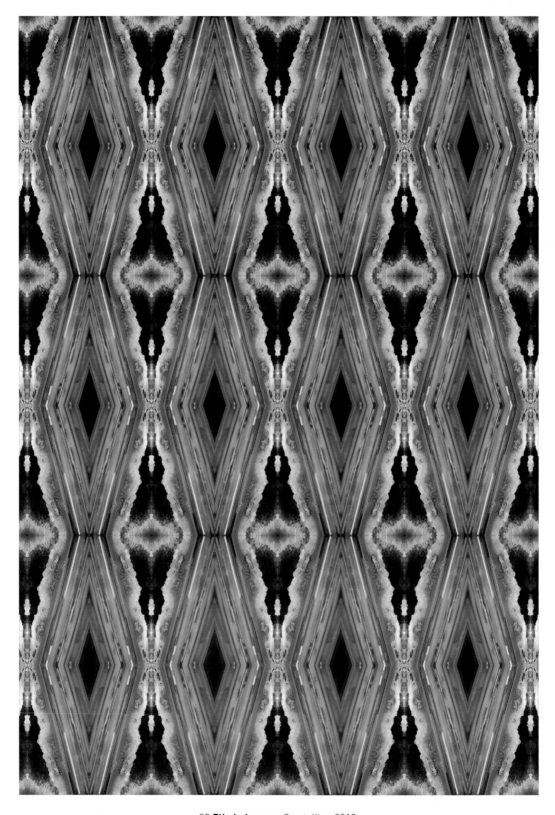

23 **Elle Lehmann**, *Crystallize*, 2012

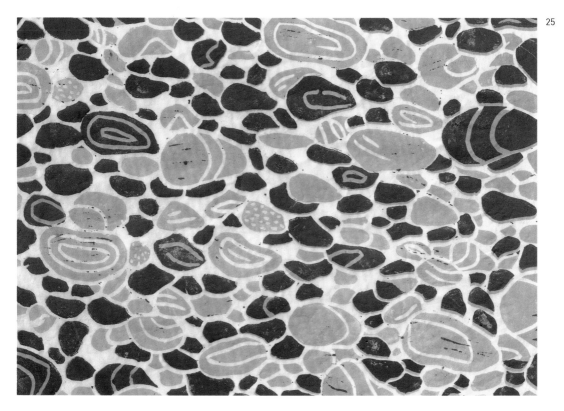

24 **April Noga | Prillamena**, *Terrace*, 2012 // 25 **Beckabonce**, *Blue Pebbles*, 2012

26 **Ursula Smith**, *Funky Flames*, 2012

27 **Connie Utterback**, *Lorenz (detail)*, 2003 // 28 *Potentia (detail)*, 2006
29 *Betula (detail)*, 2006 // 30 *Grain of Sand (detail)*, 2000

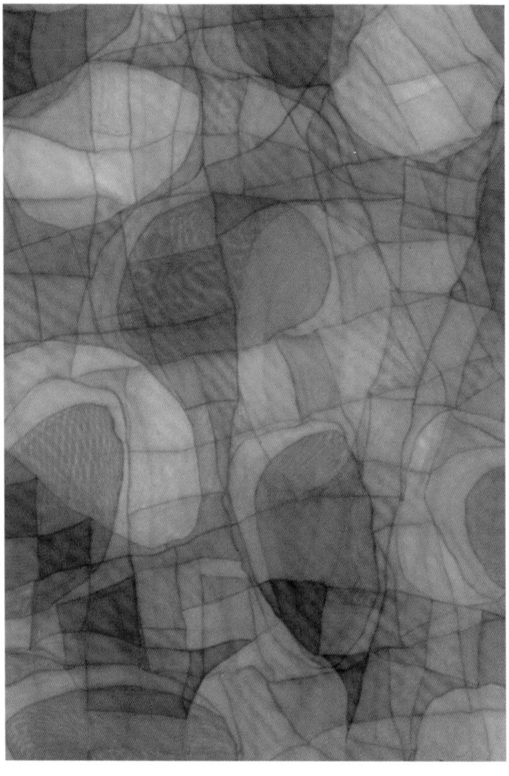

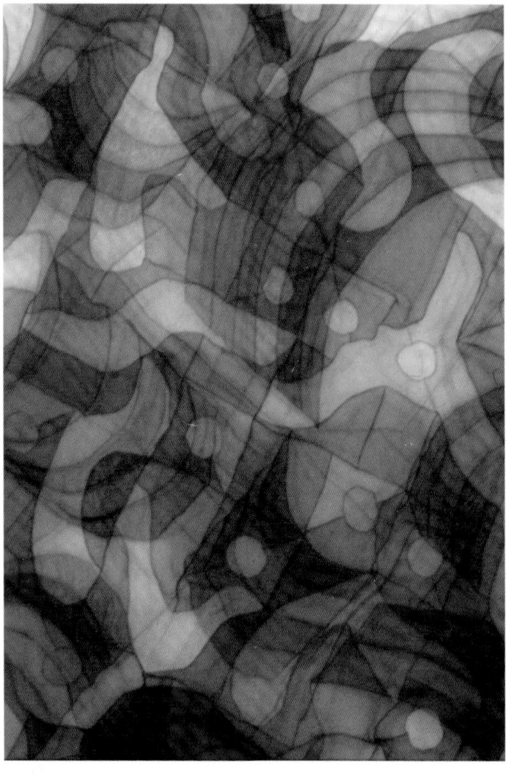

31 **Kristi O'Meara | The Patternbase**, *Hued Branches*, 2012

2

33

34

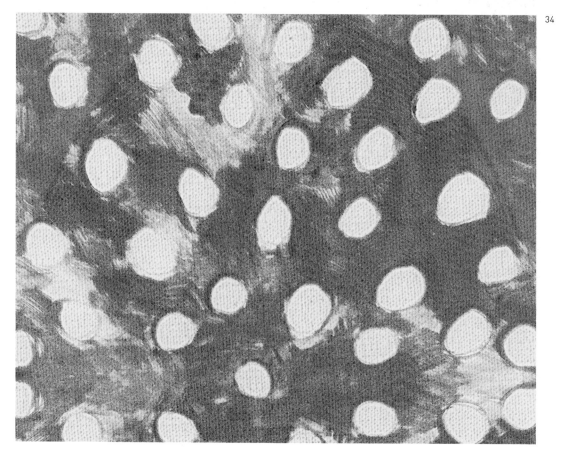

32 **Vanessa Hafezi**, *Aged 3D Floral*, 2012 // 33 **Tina Olsson | Fyllayta**, *Strawberry*, 2012
34 **Emma Formstone**, *Abstract Dash*, 2012

35 **Lynnette Miranda**, *Untitled (Pebbles)*, 2012

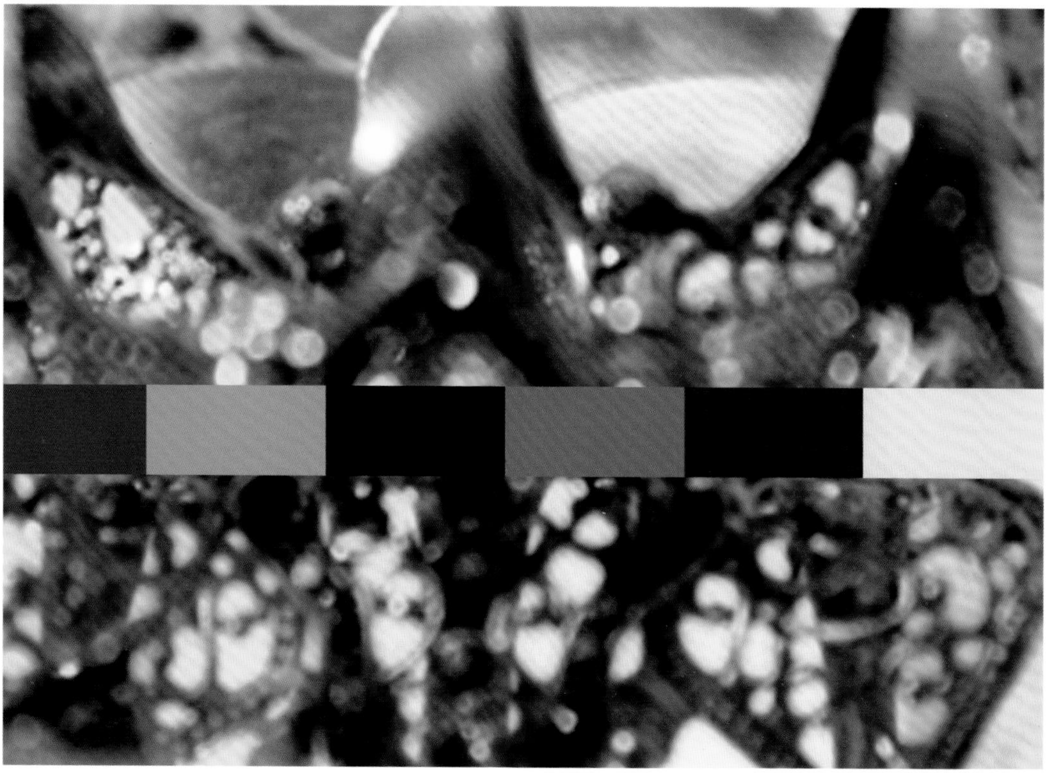

36 **Poonam Dhuffer | Maha Dhuffer**, *Maharani Multi-colour Blur*, 2011 // 37 *Maharani Blur*, 2011

38 **Lynnette Miranda**, *Untitled (Shrubs)*, 2012

39 **Naomi Hefetz**, *Undergrowth*, 2012 // 40 **Marie-Therese Wisniowski | Art Quill Studio**, *Urban Mark Making*, 2004
41 *Cultural Graffiti III*, 2004 // 42 *Casual Walls . . . Textures and Surfaces*, 2004

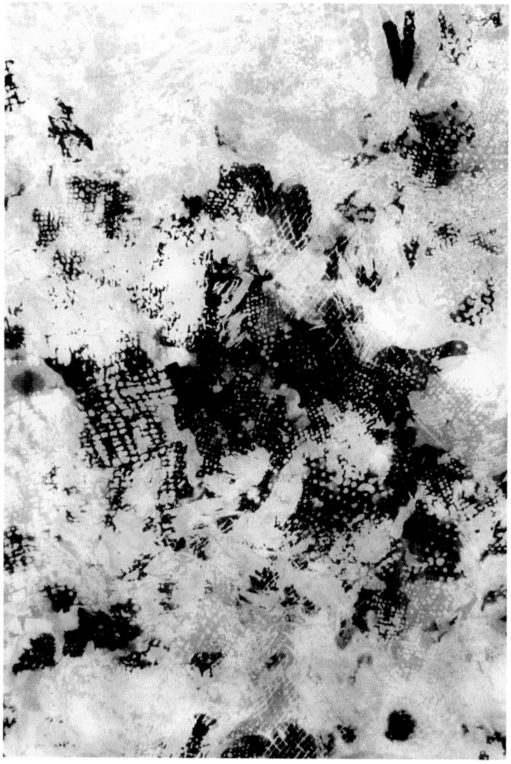

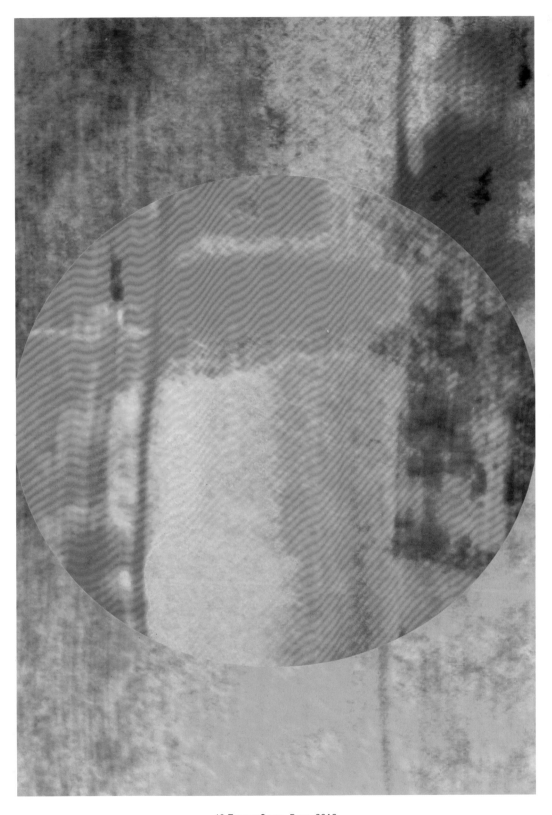

43 **Emma Cope**, *Drag*, 2012

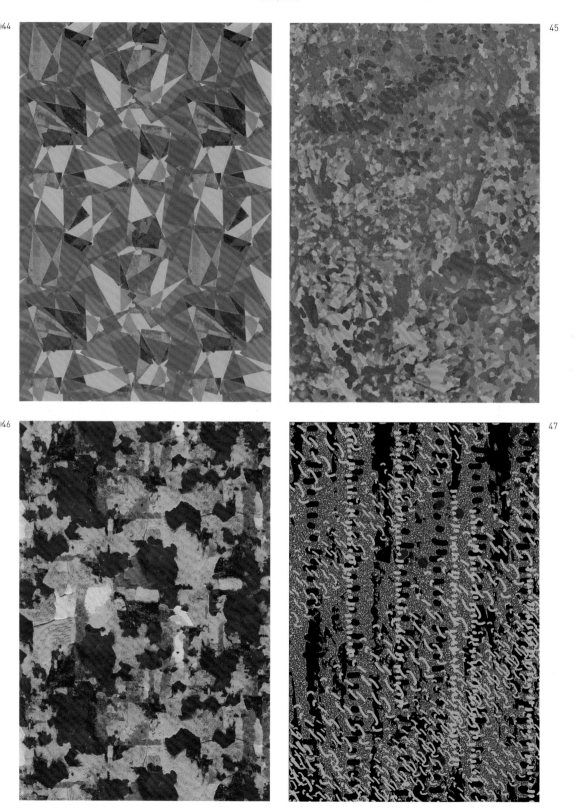

44 **Casey Mollett**, *Shard*, 2012 // 45 **Kathryn Pledger**, *Myatts Fields*, 2012
46 **Kathryn Pledger**, *Grosvenor Bark*, 2012 // 47 **Schauleh Vivian Sahba | Bouclé, SF**, *Deconstructed Tartan*, 2011

48 **Tina Olsson | Fyllayta**, *Wine and Mint*, 2012

49

50

51

52

49 **Vanessa Hafezi**, *Reflections*, 2012 // 50 **Lucy Hardcastle**, *Budgerigar*, 2012
51 **Emma Formstone**, *Confetti*, 2012 // 52 **Allure Designs**, *Transparent Leaves*, 2012

53 **Emily Jeanne Ott**, *Swan Repeat*, 2012 // 54 **Schatzi Brown by Tanya Brown**, *Mojave*, 2012
55 *Tribal 02*, 2012

56 **Schatzi Brown by Tanya Brown**, *Tribal Stripe*, 2012

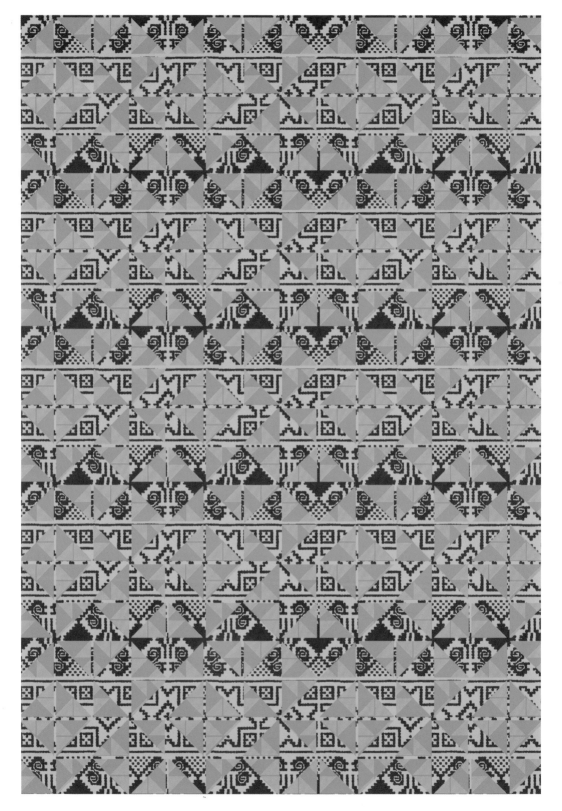

57 **Amy Jo Lewis**, *Folk Quilt*, 2012

58

59

60

61

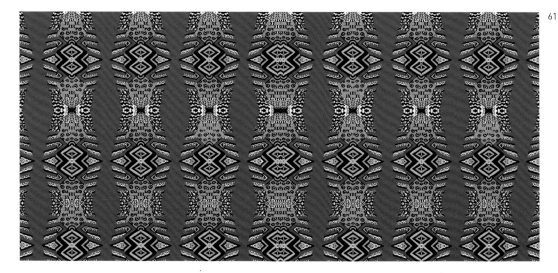

58 **Miranda Mol**, *Mexican*, 2012 // 59 *Zigzag*, 2012 // 60 **Amy Jo Lewis**, *Folk Twill*, 2012
61 **Claire Buckley**, *Tropical Waves (Hand-drawn Print)*, 2012

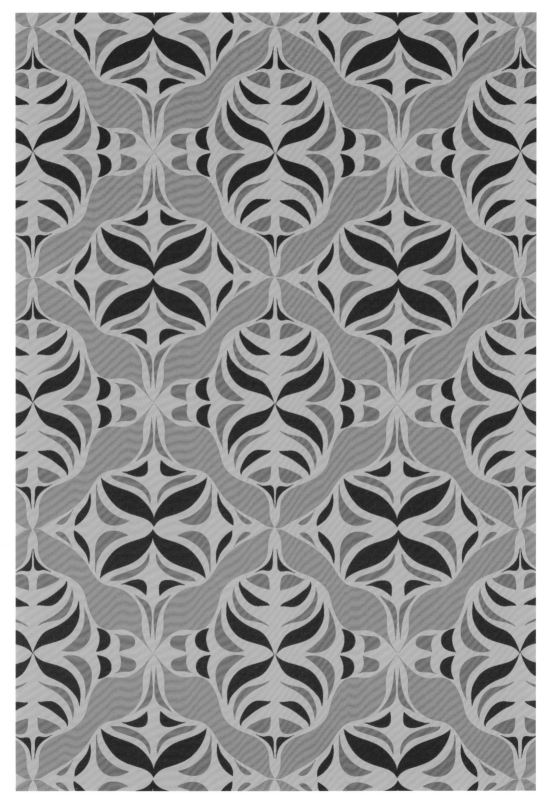

62 **Miranda Mol**, *Tangerine Tiles*, 2012

63

64

65

63, 64, 65 **Veronica Galbraith**, *Spiced Swirls*, 2012

66 **Bethan Janine**, *Kaleidoscope Flora*, 2012

67

68

69

67, 68, 69 **Lesley Merola Moya | Hunt + Gather Studio**, *Untitled*, 2012

70 **Katherina London**, *No. 14*, 2012

72

71 **Femi Ford Art & Design**, *Metamorphosis (Warm)*, 2012 // 72 *Metamorphosis (Cool)*, 2012

73

74

73 **Audrey Victoria Keiffer | The Patternbase**, *Bat*, 2012 // 74 **Claire Buckley**, *Flora & Fauna (Hand-drawn Print)*, 2012

75 **Claire Buckley**, *Geometric (Hand-drawn Print)*, 2012 // *76 Flower Blossoming (Hand-drawn Print)*, 2012

77 **Veronica Galbraith**, *The Bright Side*, 2011

78

79

80

81

78 **Jasmin Elisa Guerrero**, *Blue Forette*, 2012 // 79 **Miranda Mol**, *Mosaique*, 2012
80 **Miranda Mol**, *Twirling Paisley*, 2012 // 81 **Jasmin Elisa Guerrero**, *Blue Tiles*, 2012

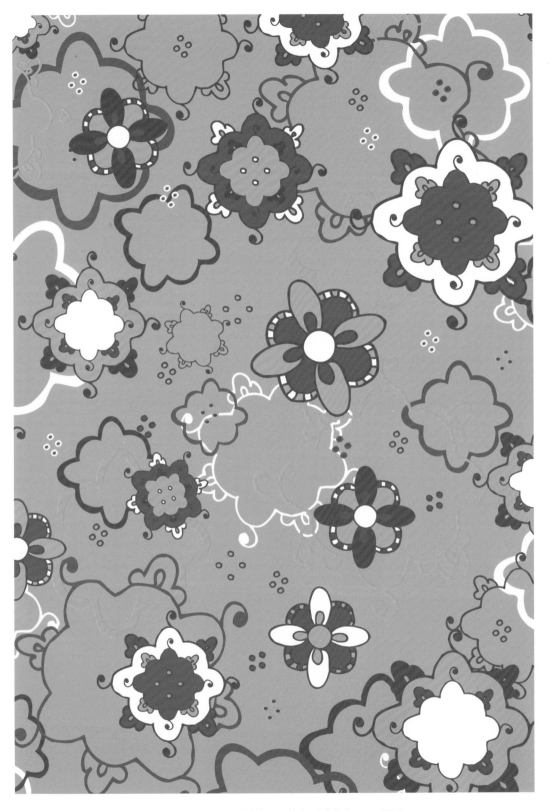

82 **Justine Aldersey-Williams**, *Mehndi Folk Orange*, 2012

83

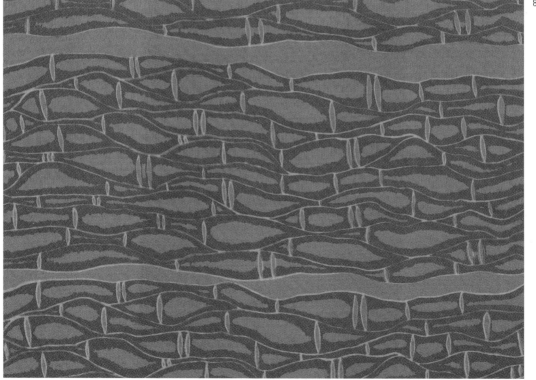

84

83 **Tina Olsson | Fyllayta**, *Solar Flare*, 2012 // 84 **Bets Kumor**, *Chinese Maple*, 2010

85

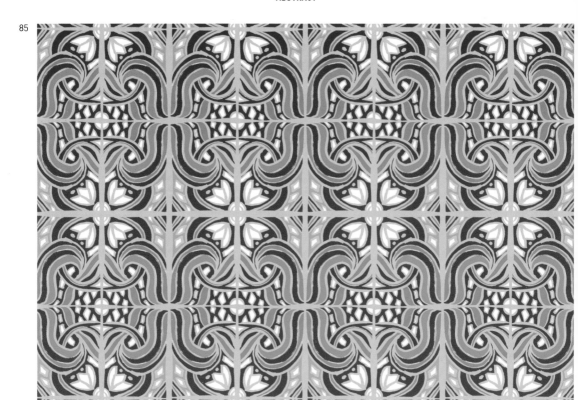

86

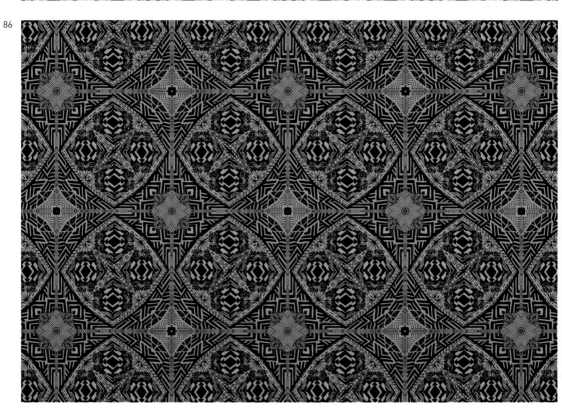

85 **Femi Ford Art & Design**, *Blue Wave*, 2012 // 86 **Claire Buckley**, *Stars and Stripes (Hand-drawn Print)*, 2012

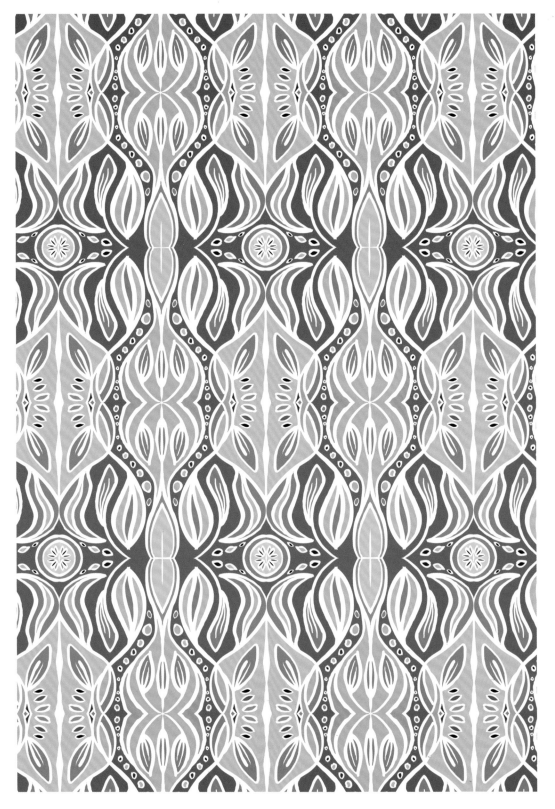

87 **Femi Ford Art & Design**, *Ocean Migration*, 2012

88 **Martin Leon | Male ®**, *Kamasutra 4*, 2011

89 **Martin Leon | Male ®**, *Kamasutra 6*, 2011 // 90 *Kamasutra 5*, 2011
91 *Kamasutra 1*, 2011 // 92 *Kamasutra 3*, 2011 // 93 *Kamasutra 2*, 2011

94 **Marta Spendowska**, *Geometric Droplets*, 2012

95 **Jasmin Elisa Guerrero**, *Sevilla 5*, 2012 // 96 **MaJoBV by Maria José Bautista V**, *Celebration Lights*, 2012
97 **Erin Wootten | erinandmarie**, *Object, Found*, 2012 // 98 **Taylor Telyan**, *Hunting Fur*, 2012

1 **Audrey Victoria Keiffer | The Patternbase**, *Lush*, 2012

2 **Audrey Victoria Keiffer | The Patternbase**, *Flamingo Finale*, 2012 // 3 *Square*, 2012
4 *Luna*, 2012 // 5 *Child's Play*, 2012 // 6 *Kaleidodress*, 2012

7 **Schauleh Vivian Sahba | Bouclé, SF**, *Cloud Lines*, 2012

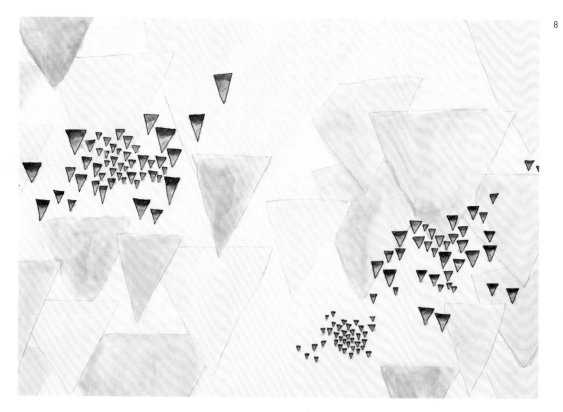

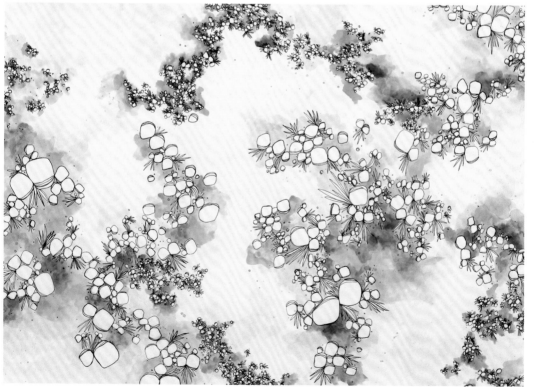

8 **April Noga | Prillamena**, *Candy Corn*, 2012 // *9 Holly*, 2012

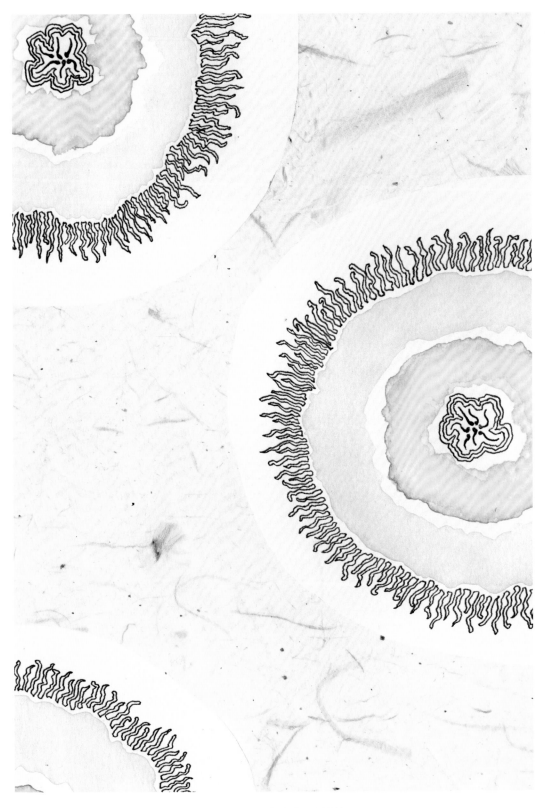

10 **Vanessa Hafezi**, *Coral*, 2011

11 **Vanessa Hafezi**, *Bamboo*, 2011

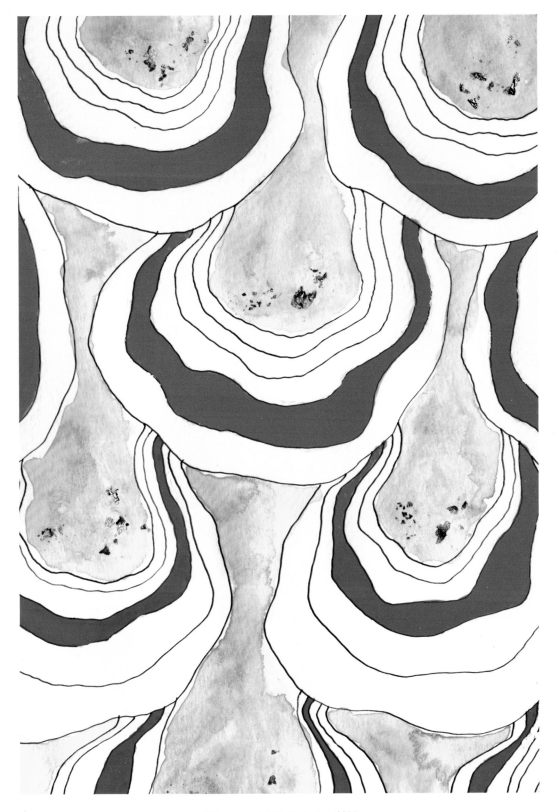

12 **Vanessa Hafezi**, *Radiation*, 2011

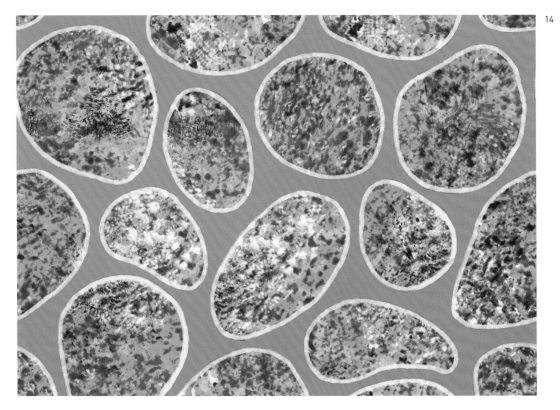

13 **April Noga | Prillamena**, *Summer Licks*, 2009 // 14 **Kristi O'Meara | The Patternbase**, *Red Marbled Pebbles*, 2012

15 **Lucy Hardcastle**, *Kingfisher*, 2012

16 **MaJoBV by Maria José Bautista V**, *Doodled Weave*, 2012 // 17 **Saberah Malik**, *Culterations*, 2002
18 **MaJoBV by Maria José Bautista V**, *Doodled Checks*, 2012 // 19 **April Noga | Prillamena**, *Starflakes*, 2011

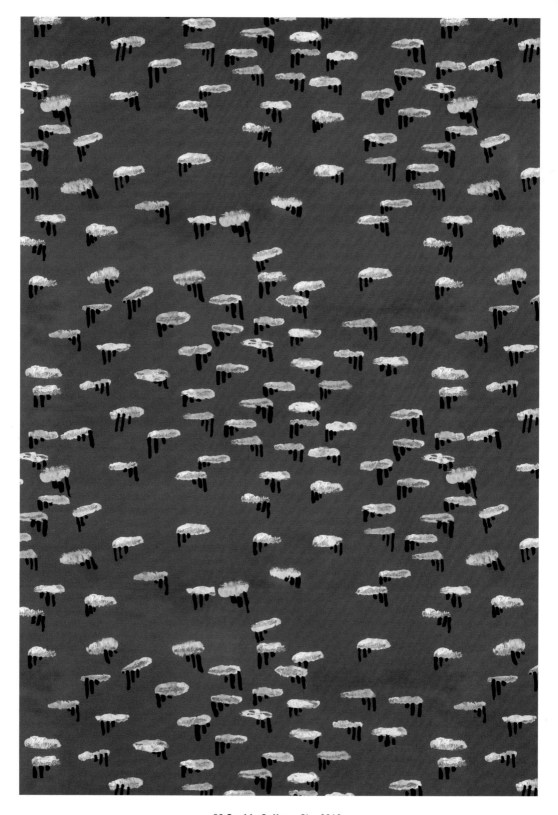

20 **Sophie Collom**, *Sky*, 2012

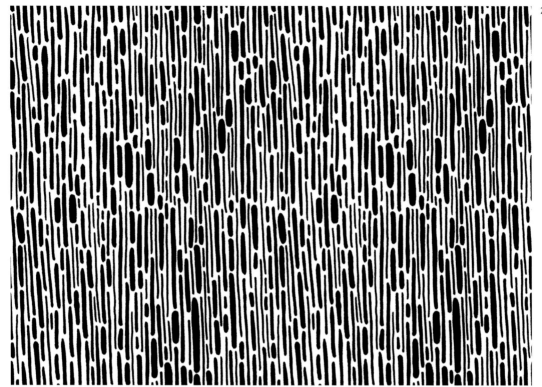

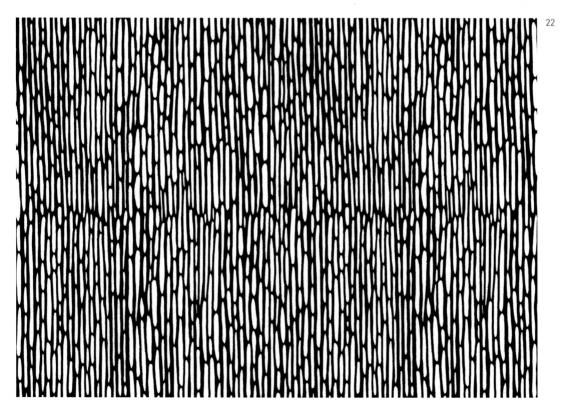

21, 22 **Kristi O'Meara | The Patternbase**, *Dashed Lines (Black on White)*, 2012

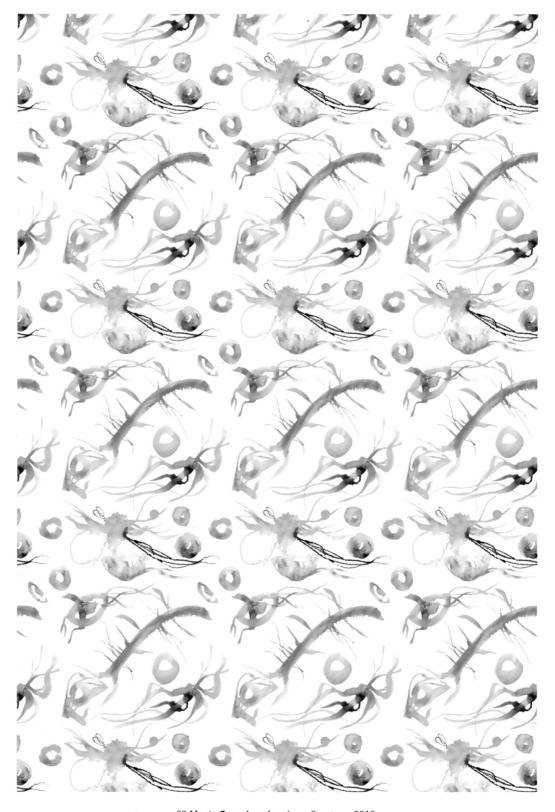

23 **Marta Spendowska**, *Aqua Creature*, 2012

24

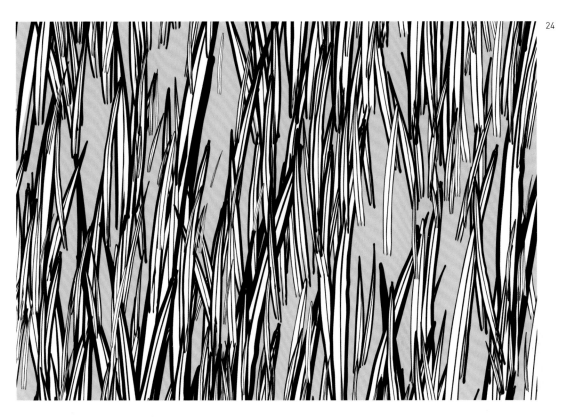

25

24 **Katy Clemmans | Surface Pattern Design**, *Long Grass*, 2012
25 **MaJoBV by Maria José Bautista V**, *Constellation Feathers*, 2012

26 **Audrey Victoria Keiffer | The Patternbase**, *Wing*, 2013

27 **Audrey Victoria Keiffer | The Patternbase**, *Genie*, 2013

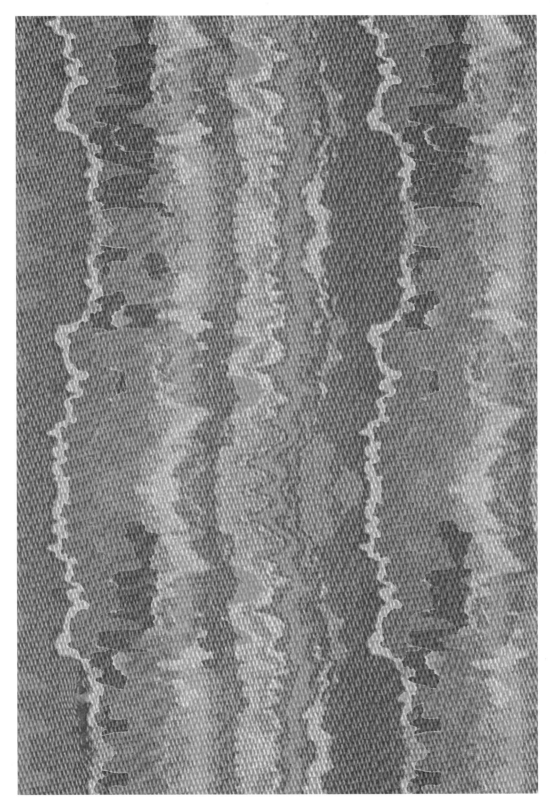

28 **Emma Formstone**, *Blurred Lines*, 2012

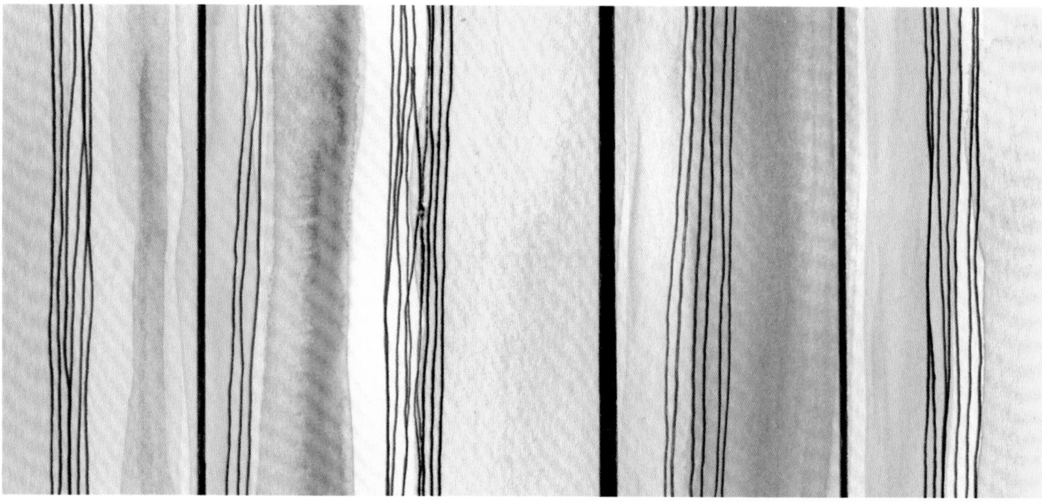

29 **Vanessa Hafezi**, *Candystripe*, 2011 // 30 **Emma Formstone**, *Colourdash*, 2012
31 **Casey Mollett**, *Tension*, 2011 // 32 **Chelsea Densmore**, *Canyon Stripe*, 2012

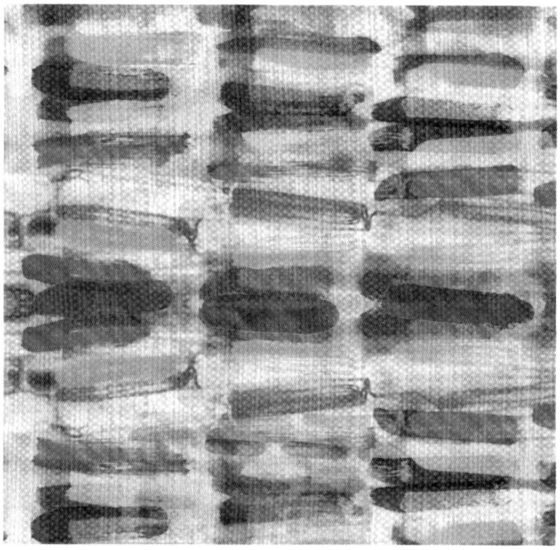

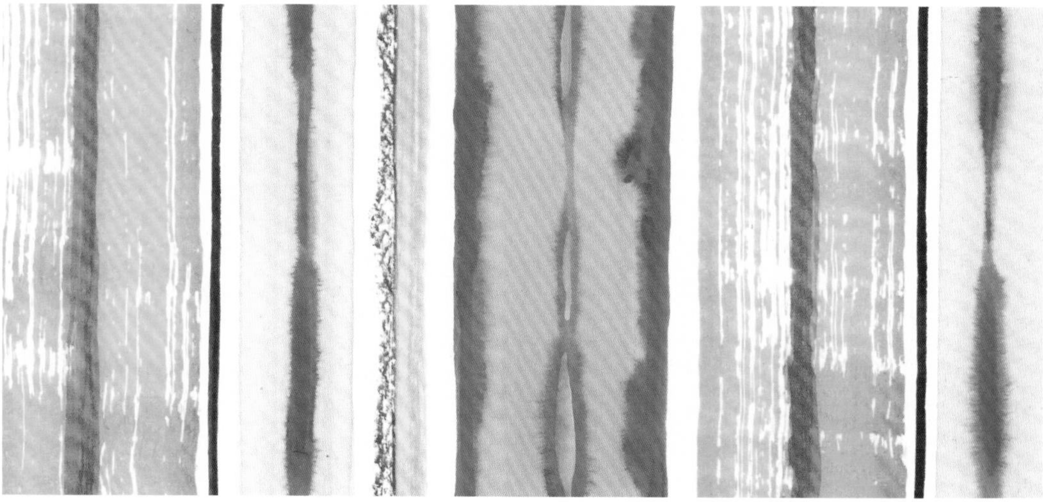

33 **Emma Formstone**, *Coloured Splatter*, 2012

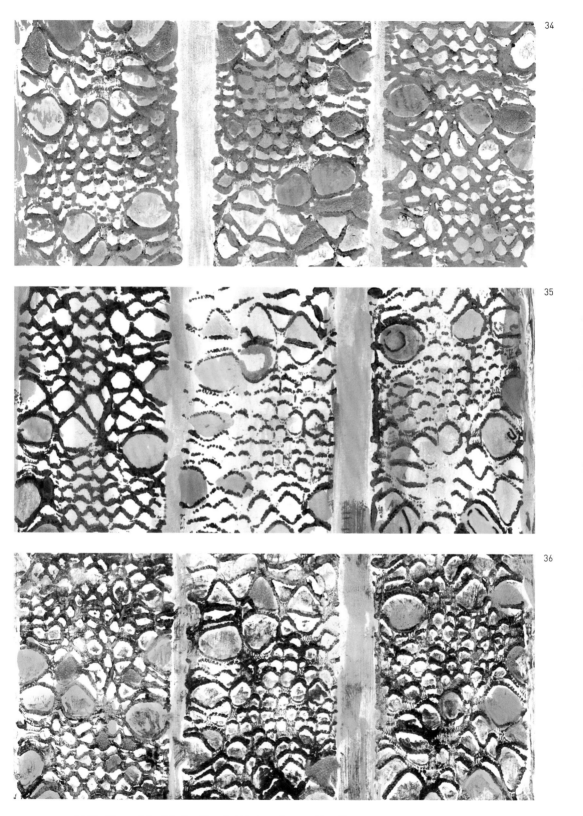

34 **Zia Gipson | Art Isle Studios**, *Bubble Lace Spring*, 2012 // 35 *Bubble Lace Marine*, 2012
36 *Bubble Lace Midnight*, 2012

37 **Naomi Hefetz**, *Forced Nature*, 2012

38 **Naomi Hefetz**, *Chained*, 2012

39 **Ingrid Johnson**, *Bleach Flowers*, 2012

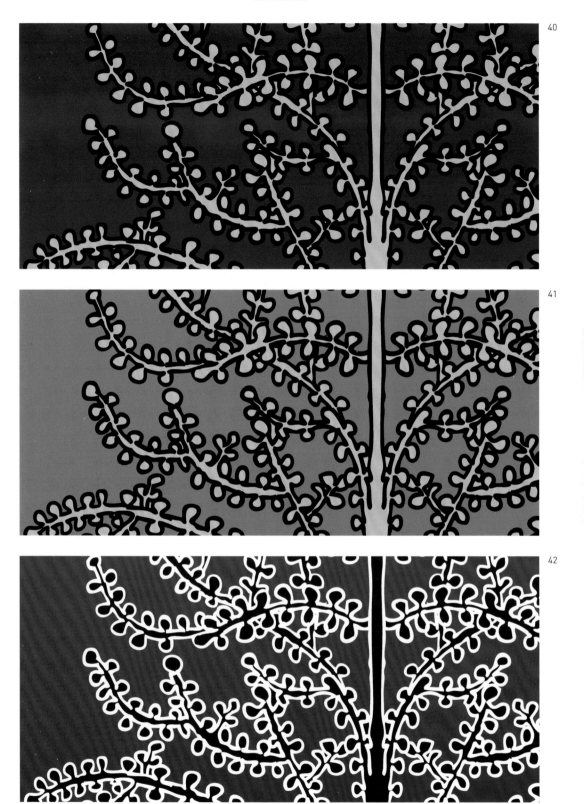

40 **Simi Gauba**, *Rudra-hara*, 2012 // 41 *Rudra-sarson*, 2012 // 42 *Rudra-neel*, 2012

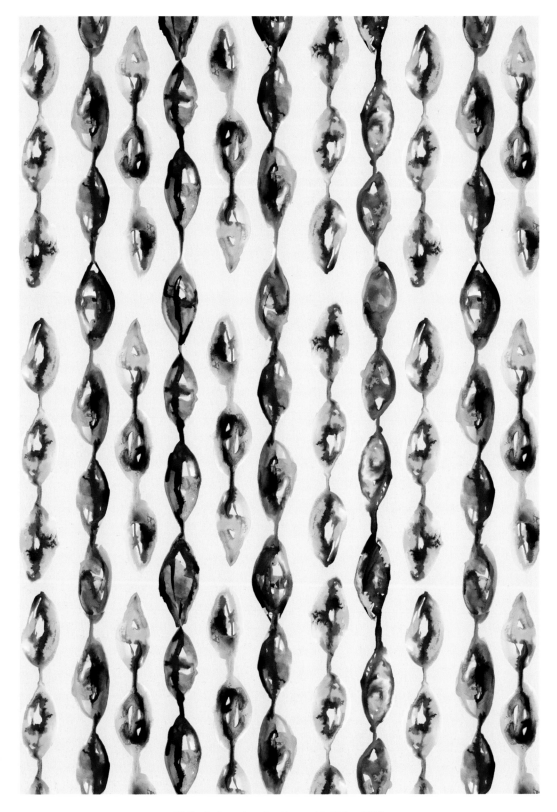

43 **Marta Spendowska**, *Geometric Water*, 2012

44

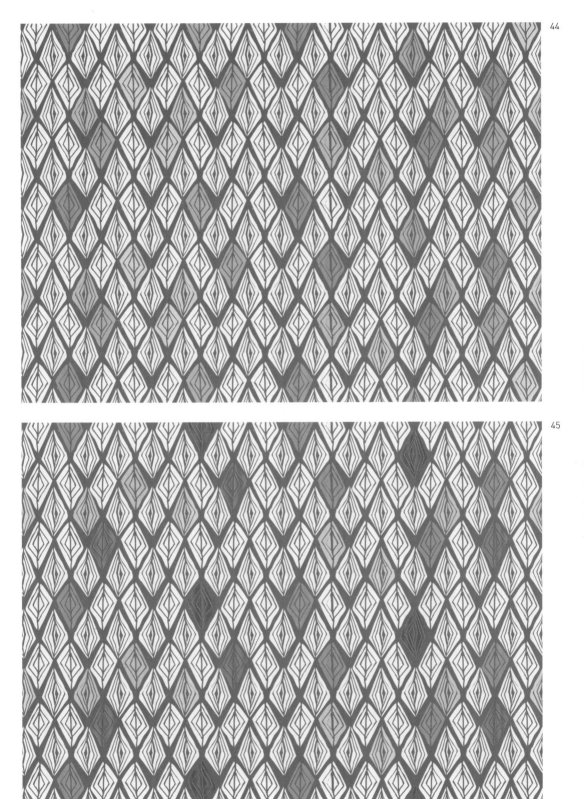

45

44 Femi Ford Art & Design, *Some Days are Diamonds (Cool)*, 2012 // 45 *Some Days are Diamonds (Warm)*, 2012

46 **Dustin Williams**, *Breaking News: Creaky Floorboards Still Creepy*, 2012

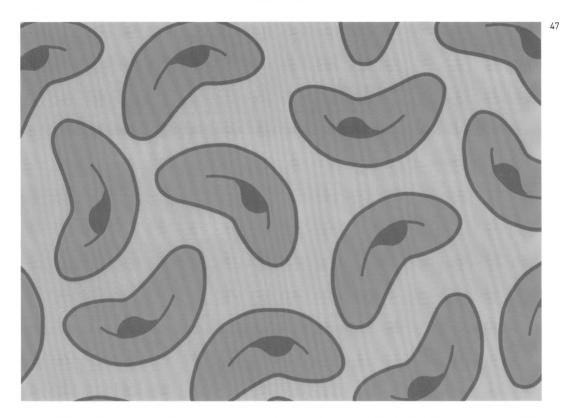

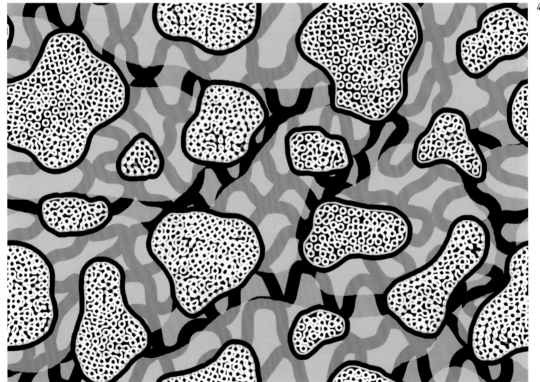

47 **Taylor Telyan**, *Bigmouth*, 2011 // 48 **Kristi O'Meara | The Patternbase**, *Plasma*, 2013

49

50

51

52

53

49 **Sian Elin**, *Create and Scribble*, 2012 // 50 **Brenda Sutton | Bren Michelle Design**, *Retro Televisions – Grey and Teal*, 2012
51 *Retro Televisions – Mustard*, 2012 // 52 **Sian Elin**, *London*, 2012 // 53 **Brenda Sutton | Bren Michelle Design**, *Retro Televisions – Pink and Mint*, 2012

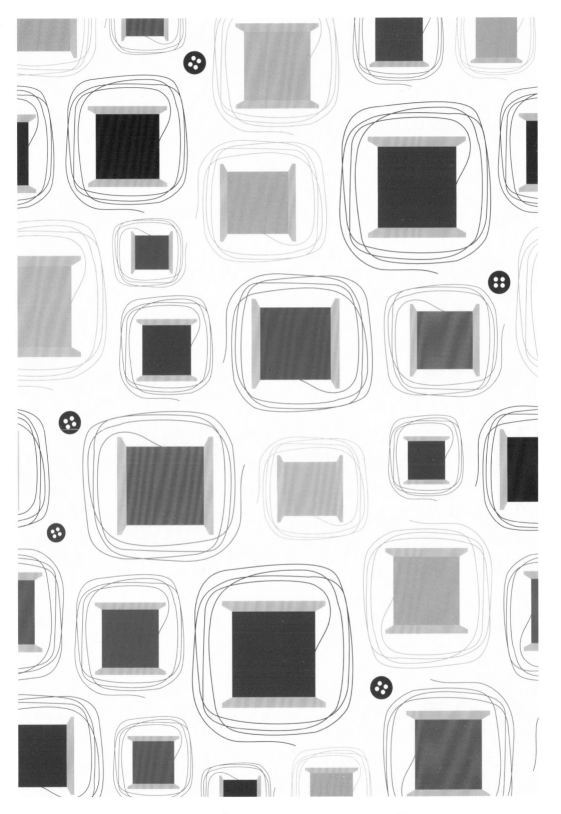

54 **Brenda Sutton | Bren Michelle Design**, *Cotton Reels*, 2011

55 **Jaquelina Freitas**, *Rain*, 2010

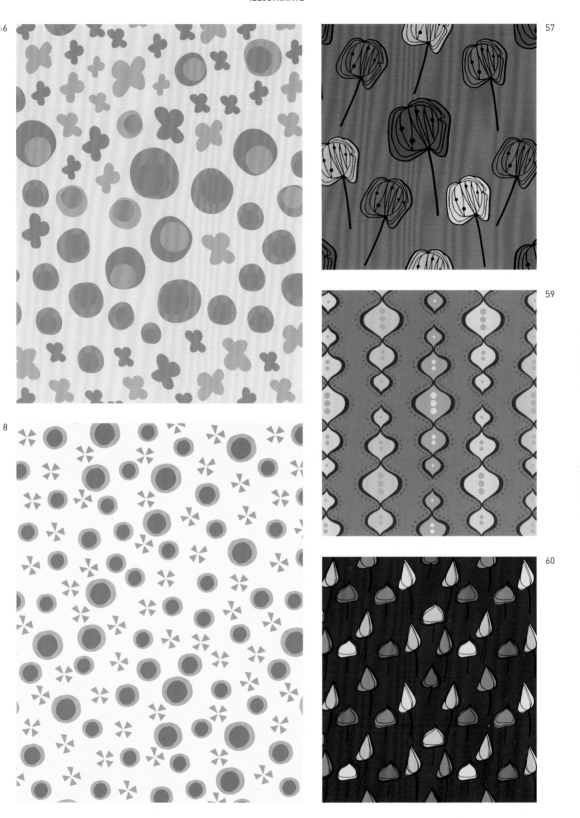

56 **Rachel Gresham Design**, *Circle Romp Ditty*, 2012 // 57 **Allure Designs**, *Flowers on Sticks*, 2012 // 58 **Rachel Gresham Design**, *Town Square Beige*, 2012 // 59 **Liz Smith | Elle Jane Designs**, *Lilac Pendant*, 2012 // 60 **Allure Designs**, *Wild Tulips*, 2012

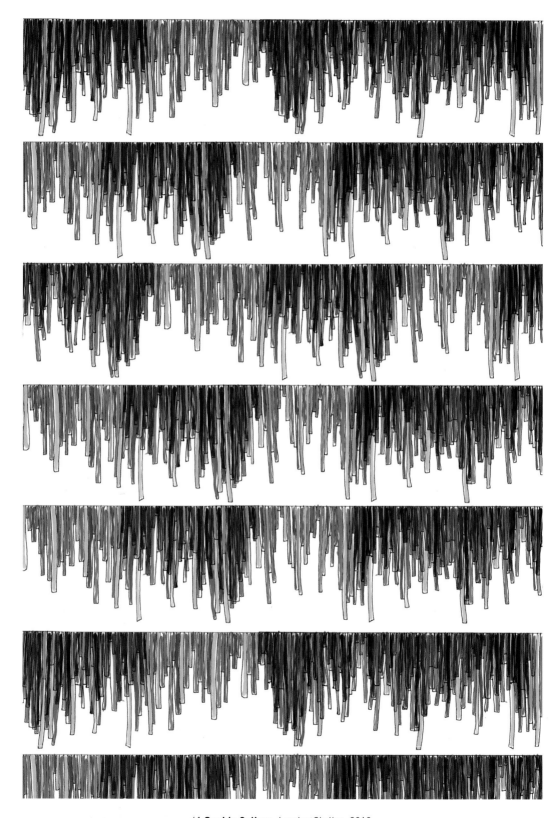

61 **Sophie Collom**, *London Skyline*, 2012

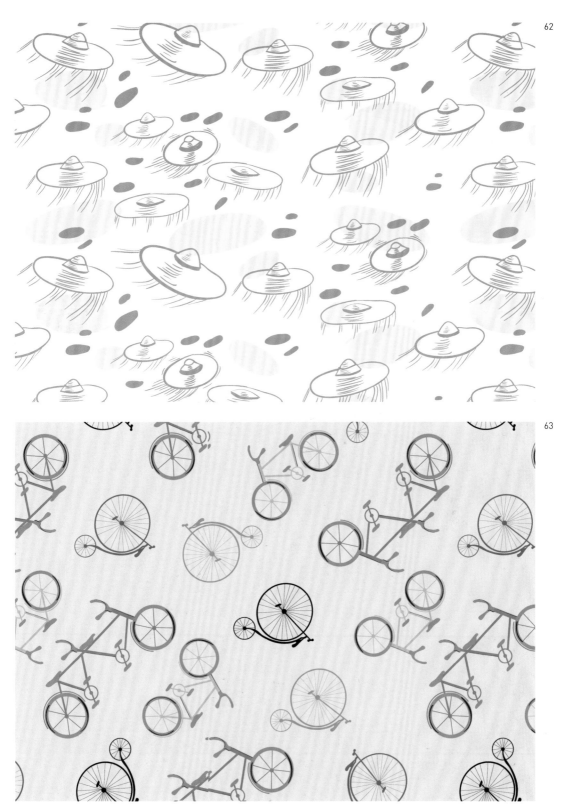

62 **Olivia Mew**, *Ufos*, 2012 // 63 **Jennifer D'Eugenio**, *Neutral Bikes*, 2012

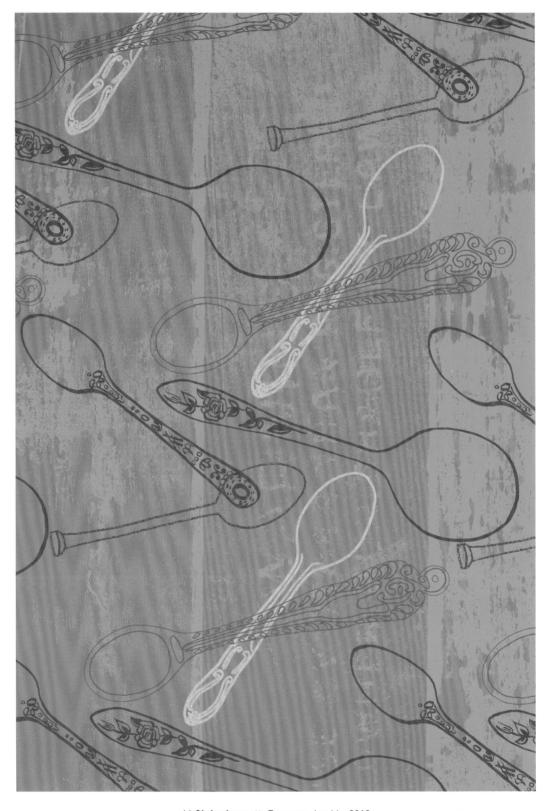

64 **Claire Leggett**, *Teaspoon Jumble*, 2012

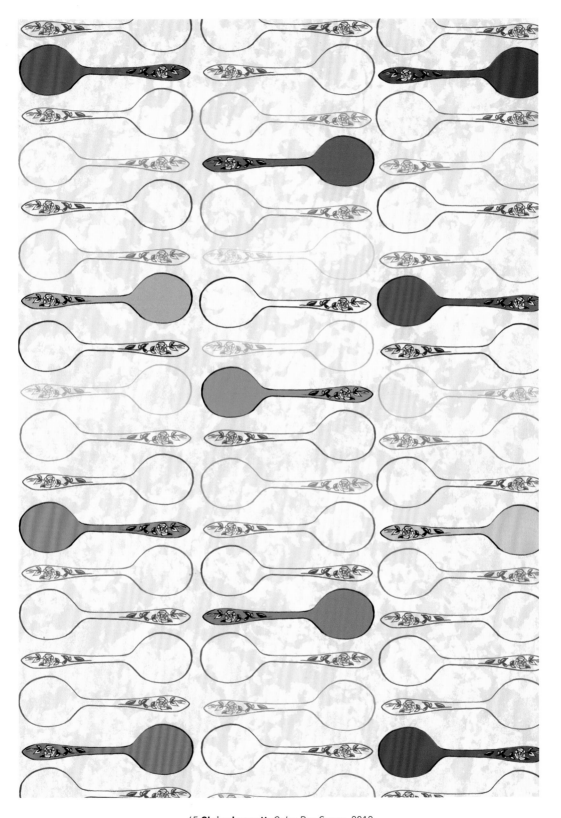

65 **Claire Leggett**, *Color Pop Spoon*, 2012

66 **Natalie Alexander**, *Lace Hearts*, 2013

67

68

69

67 **Jennie Whitham of JLW Illustration**, *Electric Interlope – Lace*, 2012 // 68 *Electric Interlope – Patchwork*, 2012
69 **CJ Hungerman**, *Cosmo Robotica*, 2012

70 **Anna Oguienko**, *Broken Herringbone*, 2012

71 **Dawn Clarkson**, *Love Leaves*, 2012

Kristi O'Meara | **The Patternbase**, *Swatches*, 2013

7 // Fabric Swatches

1 **Louise Mills Textiles**, *Double Cloth Neon/Neutral Collection*, 2007

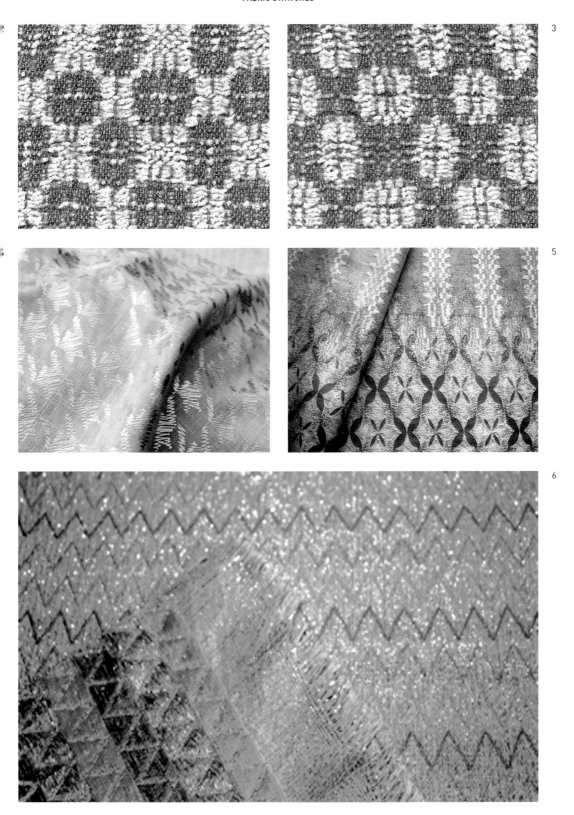

2 **Kristen Pickell | Woven Nostalgia**, *Pink and Gold #1*, 2009 // 3 *Pink and Gold #2*, 2009 // 4 **Janna Roküsek**, *Sloane collection, Spring/Summer 2013*, 2012 // 5 **Amy Jo Lewis**, *Lace Coverlet*, 2011 // 6 **Louise Mills Textiles**, *Fashion Fabric Shetland Sunset*, 2011

7

8

7, 8 **Etta Sandry**, *A Scale of Opinions in Blue and Orange*, 2012

10

11

9 **Louise Mills Textiles**, *Double Cloth Bricks*, 2007 // 10 **Dan Riley & Jeannine Han**, *'Untitled' from the body of work called 'Textilen and the Electric Ribbon' by Dan Riley & Jeannine Han*, 2010 // 11 **Roshannah Bagley**, *Rutu*, 2009

12 **Senyor Pablo**, *Cones Jacquard Detail*, 2012

3

14

15

13 **Della Reams, co-designed with AlDana Al Khater**, *Aldana Fabric*, 2011 (the motif spells AlDana in Arabic)
14 **Della Reams, co-designed with Nada Hammada**, *Nada Fabric*, 2011 (the motif spells Nada in Arabic)
15 **Della Reams, co-designed with Basra Bashir**, *Basra Fabric*, 2011 (the motif spells Basra in Arabic)

16 **Senyor Pablo**, *Cones Jacquard (detail)*, 2012

17

18

19

20

21

22

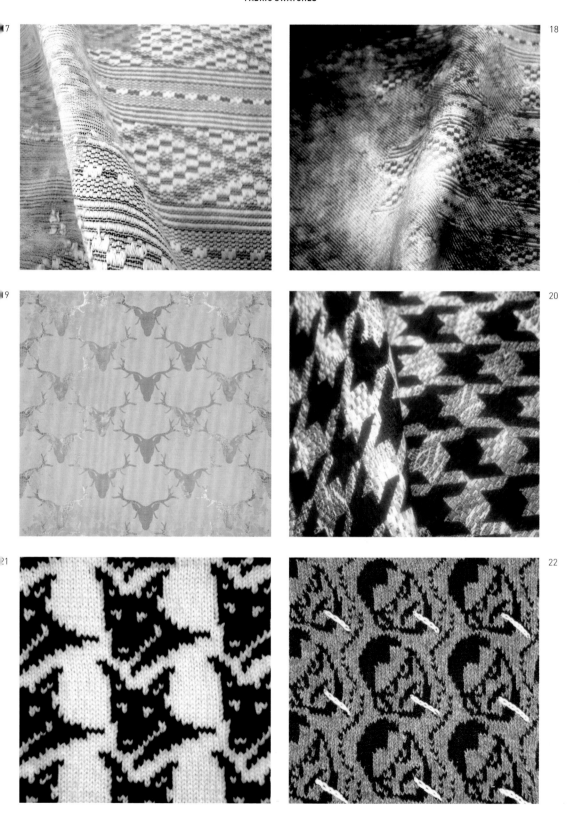

17 **Amy Jo Lewis**, *Degraded Shirting*, 2011 // 18 **Amy Jo Lewis**, *Gradated Coverlet*, 2011
19 **Michelle Manolov | Pattern and Co**, *Gilded Stags*, 2012 // 20 **Amy Jo Lewis**, *Houndstooth Coverlet*, 2011
21 **Della Reams**, *Houndstooth Hound Fabric*, 2009 // 22 **Della Reams**, *The Smoker Fabric*, 2009

23 **Jasmin Elisa Guerrero**, *Clouds*, 2008

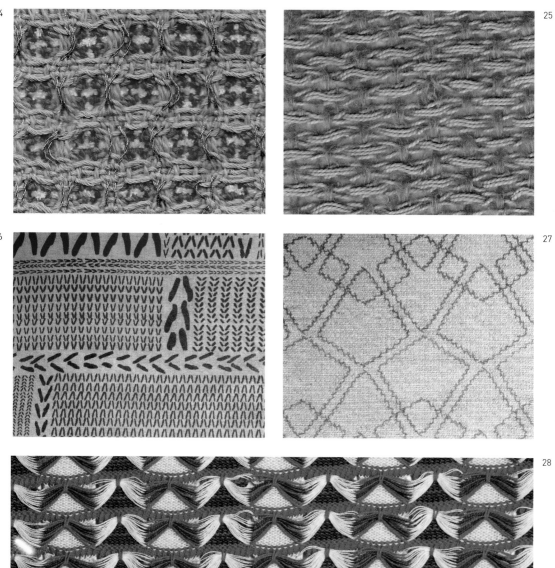

24 **Kristen Pickell | Woven Nostalgia**, *Finale*, 2010 // 25 *Green*, 2008 // 26 **Taylor Telyan**, *Postal Service*, 2011
27 *Space Signals*, 2011 // 28 **Dan Riley & Jeannine Han**, *'Untitled' from the body of work called 'Textilen and the Electric Ribbon'*
by Dan Riley & Jeannine Han, 2010

29 **Marcia L. Weiss**, *Dialogue II*, 2011

30

31

32

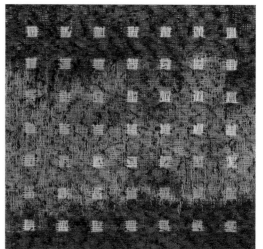

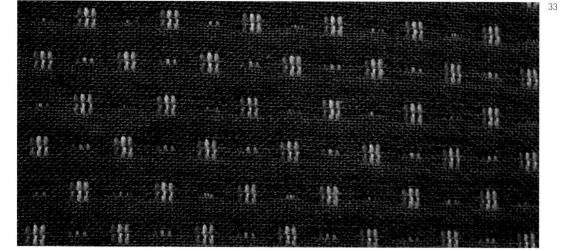

33

30, 31 **Simi Gauba**, *Mira*, 2010 // 32 **Marcia L. Weiss**, *Ethnicity*, 2011 // 33 **Simi Gauba**, *Mira*, 2010

34 Susan Johnson | Avalanche Looms, *We're Not out of the Woods Yet #4*, 2013 // 35 *We're Not out of the Woods Yet #1*, 2012
36 *We're Not out of the Woods Yet #2*, 2012 // 37 *We're Not out of the Woods Yet #3*, 2013

38 **Cantoinette Studios**, *Sister Queen! Sister Queen!*, 2011

39

40

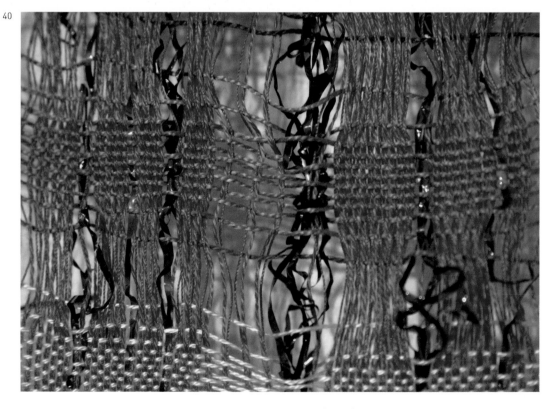

39, 40 **Etta Sandry**, *Party Fabric (detail)*, 2012

41

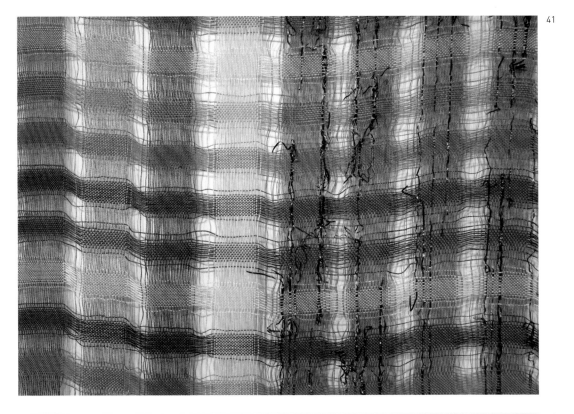

42

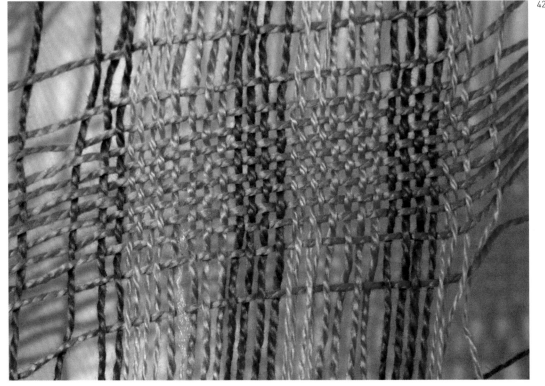

41, 42 **Etta Sandry**, *Party Fabric (detail)*, 2012

43 **Nelda Warkentin**, *Summer Walk*, 2005

44

45

44 **Roshannah Bagley**, *Buds (Series)*, 2009 // 45 *Basillica (Repeat)*, 2010

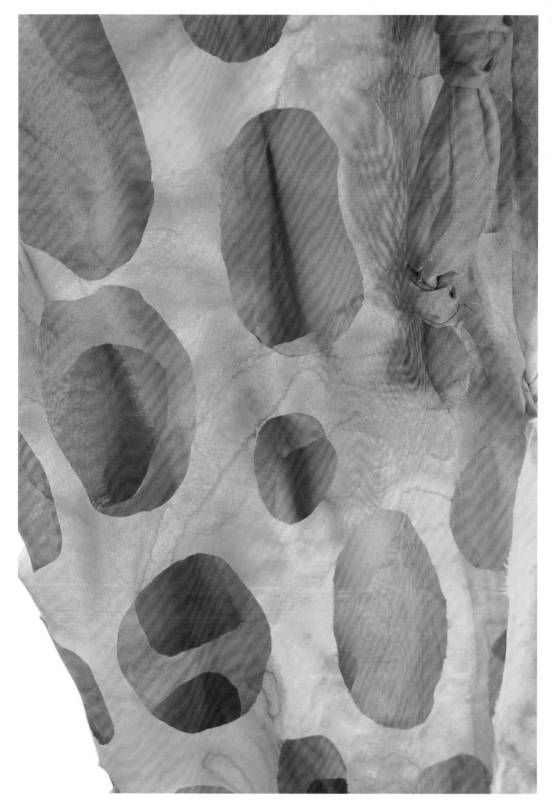

46 **Jane Ogren**, *JEFO #622*, 2009

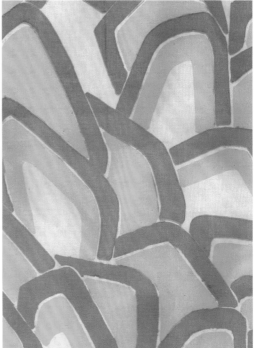

47 **Taylor Telyan**, *Rounded*, 2011 // 48 **Michele Castellano**, *Peaks*, 2011 // 49 **Bets Kumor**, *Rivers*, 2011

50 **Hannah Thayer Johnson**, *Pentaquilt (detail)*, 2010

51

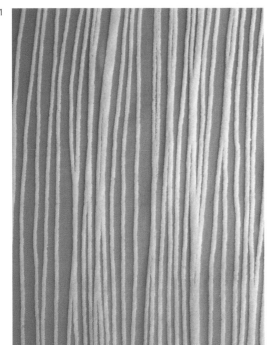

52

53

51 **Alyse Czack**, *Furrow*, 2012 // 52 **Gwyned Trefethen**, *Hope Springs Eternal (detail)*, 2006
53 **Jane Ogren**, *Mixed Media #224 (Circles 2)*, 2010

54 **Garry Noland**, *Zipper (detail)*, 2011

55

56

57

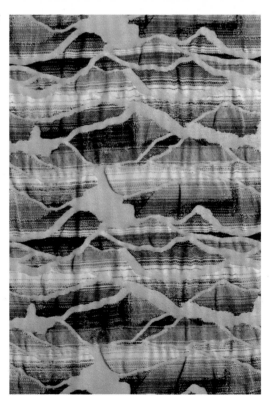

58

55 **Victoria Martinez**, *La Unica Taqueria Granted Gold*, 2012
56 **Victoria Martinez**, *21st Place Mural, Repeated Revelations*, 2012
57 **Andrea C. Purcell**, *Hills of Newspaper*, 2012 // 58 **Garry Noland**, *Twirl*, 2010

59 **Saberah Malik**, *Forestations*, 2012

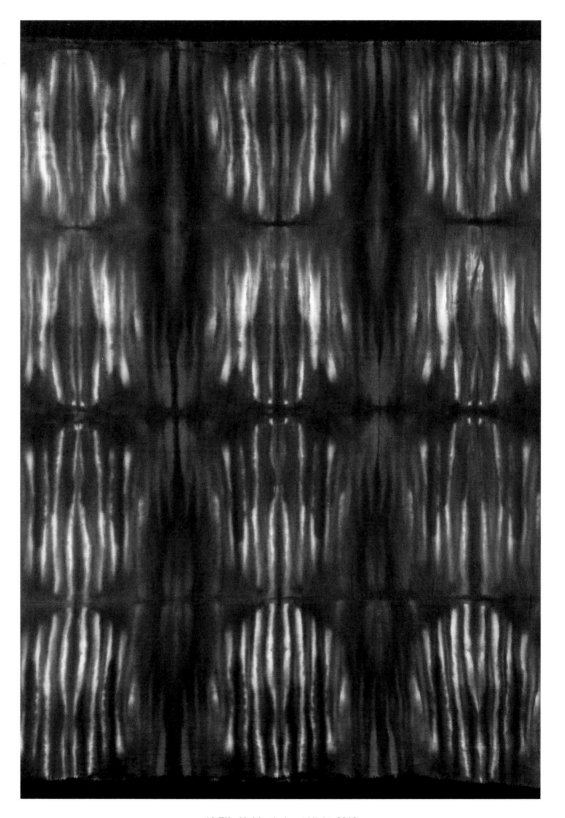

60 **Elin Noble**, *Lake at Night*, 2012

61 **Elin Noble**, *Fugitive Pieces 3*, 2011

62

63

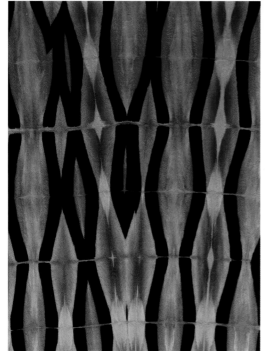 

64

62 **Elin Noble**, *Figurative Pieces 7*, 2011 // 63 **Elin Noble**, *Fugitive Pieces 9*, 2012 // 64 **Daniela Guarin**, *Tao l*, 2012

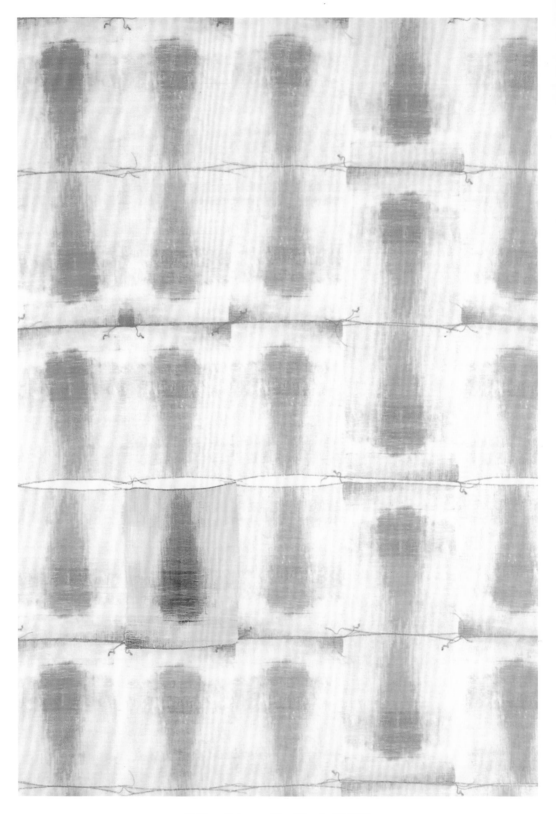

65 **Diana Palermo**, *Visual Puzzle #3*, 2010

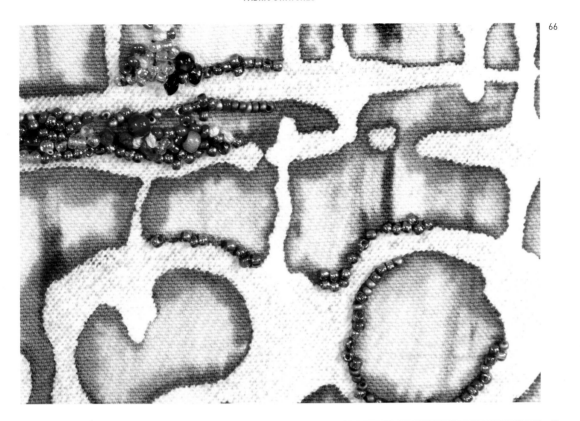

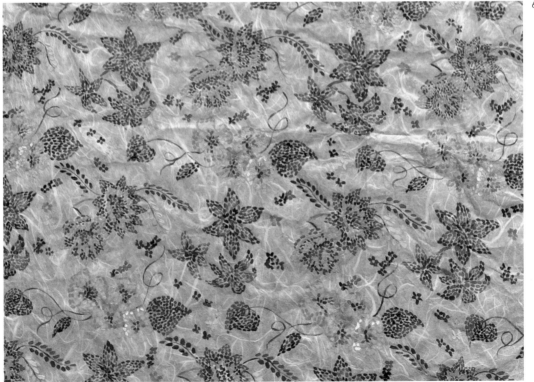

66 **Jane Ogren**, *Mixed Media #218*, 2008 // 67 **Daniela Guarin**, *Garden Paradise*, 2011

68

69

68 **Krista Jo Mustain**, *Geometric Wall Hanging (detail)*, 2011 // 69 *Coral Quilt (detail)*, 2012

70 **Amanda McCavour**, *Super-spiro-scribble Density Test, 2010* // 71 *Super-spiro-scribble Density Test (detail)*, 2010
(produced with the support of the Ontario Arts Council)

72

73

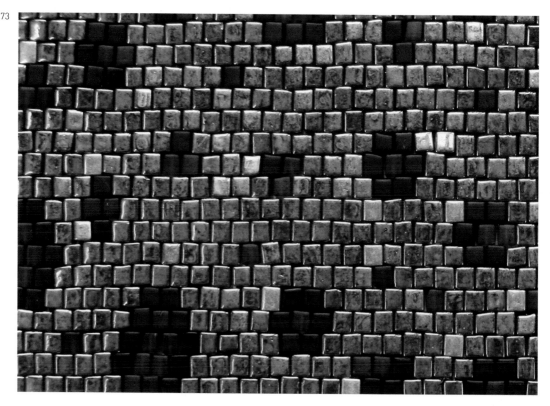

72 **Handmade by Sara Cramer**, *Pixel Pattern*, 2012 // 73 *Beaded Leopard Pattern*, 2012

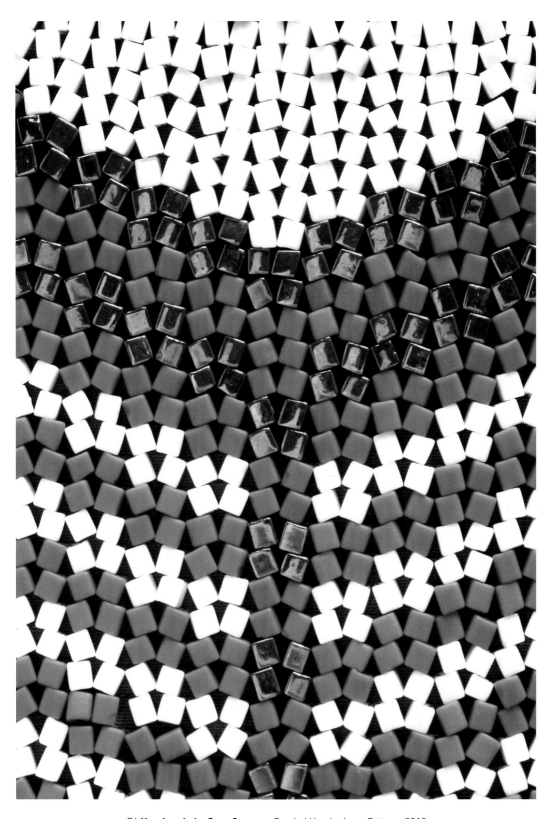

74 **Handmade by Sara Cramer**, *Beaded Herringbone Pattern*, 2012

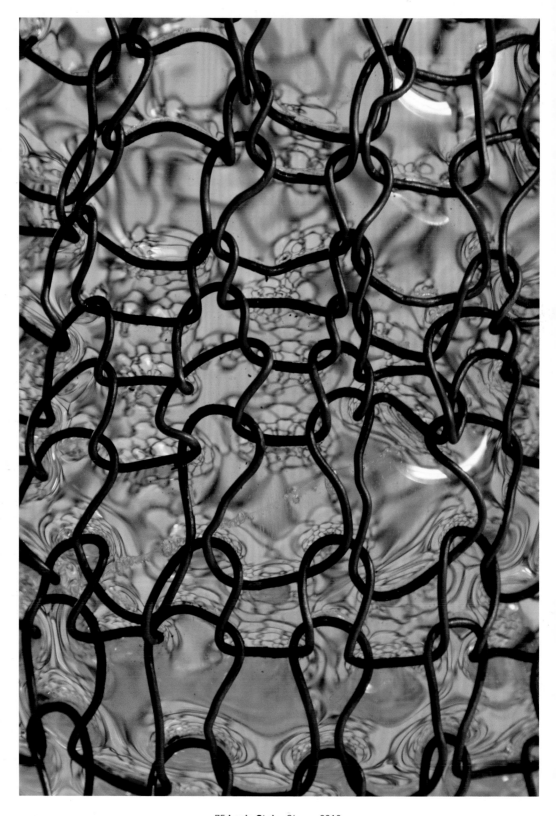

75 **Lexie Stoia**, *Glassz*, 2010

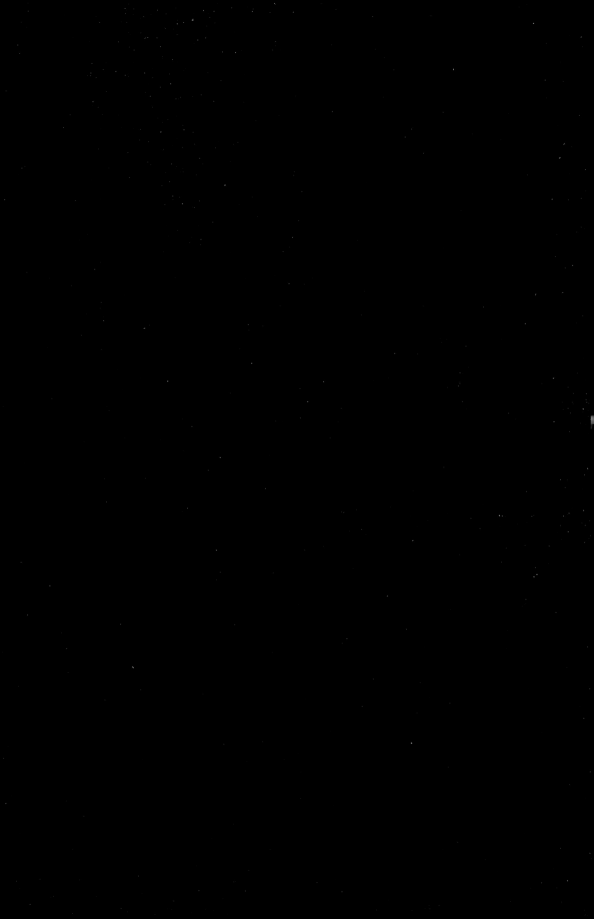

01 **Lorenzo Nanni** // 02 **Charlotte Linton** // 03 **Hannah Truran** // 04 **Senyor Pablo** // 05 **Dan Riley & Jeannine Han**
06 **Kayla Mattes** // 07 **Sabine Ducasse** // 08 **Anna-Mari Leppisaari** // 09 **Anita Hirlekar** .
10 **Jonah Jacobs** // 11 **Adrià Colorado** // 12 **String Theory** // 13 **Abby Thomas**

4

5

8

9

12

13

8 // Featured Artists

Lorenzo **Nanni**

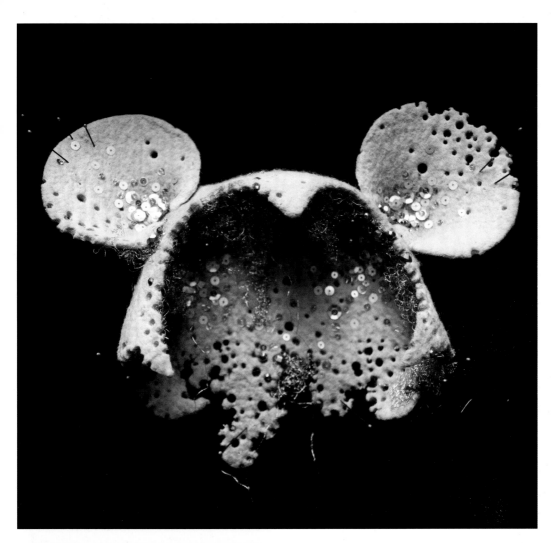

Lorenzo Nanni operates with subtlety in the realms of the beautiful and the ugly. He is inspired by botany and anatomy; his gaze is scientific and his expertly embroidered forms are surrealistic, reminding the viewer of living nature – both expressive and aggressive. Each detail is studied through a magnifying glass. Flora and fauna are reinterpreted through mutant flowers, carnivorous plants and grotesque, sprawling creatures, who thrive in felt and silk.

Nanni dissects the human body. By cutting the skin he retrieves organs and viscera that look like vibrant and precious jewelry. His work makes us travel in a phantasmagorical world, diving into the abyss of our flesh and accelerating our perception of the nature that surrounds us. The viewer will be surprised by the illusions and the contrasts that he creates.

Charlotte
Linton

Charlotte Linton is a London-based designer and illustrator. Born in Rochford, Essex in the UK, she studied Fashion Print at Central Saint Martins in London and was awarded a Masters in Printed Textiles from The Royal College of Art, London. In 2009, she launched the Charlotte Linton scarf label and has produced seasonal collections that draw inspiration from different global locations.

Linton's work has developed around the aesthetic and material potential of digitally printed textiles. She considers how such a medium can function as a carrier of content related to the roots of culture in geographically specific traditions, and in people's relationship to the flora and fauna that surround them. Each scarf has a strong visual identity that is largely illustrative, colourful and suggestive of an ongoing narrative. They are designed using a combination of hand-drawn and painted illustrations, and digital media techniques.

As a child, Linton had a keen interest in archaeology, ethnography and zoology. She created her fictional muse, Ermantrude, to collect research and take field notes on her travels across the continents. Her blog *Ermantrude's Travels* documents these zoological expeditions with imagery that often finds its way back into the scarf designs.

Since graduating, Linton has been a semi-finalist with Fashion Fringe, London, and has worked with designers such as Paul Smith, Hussein Chalayan and Chloe. Alongside her scarf collections, she has produced three

seasons of clothing and accessories for US retailer Anthropologie, under the label Zoologist by Charlotte Linton. Her work has been featured in publications such as *L'Officiel* (Paris), *The Times*, *Design Bureau*, *Arise* magazine and on websites such as vogue.com, refinery29.com, dailycandy.com and coolhunting.com.

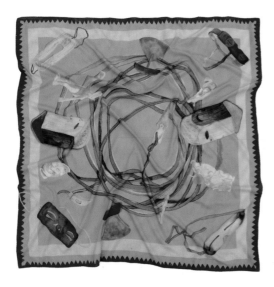

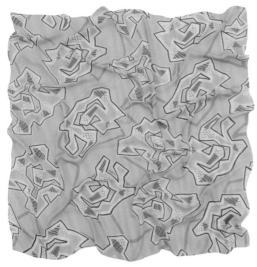

Hannah **Truran**

Hannah Truran is a London-based textile designer/maker who specializes in prints. Originally trained in illustration, Truran was drawn to textiles because of her desire to create her fantasy world. After several years of working on textile designs for interiors, she finally had the chance to explore this intensively during her masters studies at the Royal College of Art in London.

Her graduation collection 'Volstar' is a set of body pieces designed for a futuristic warrior huntress. Inspired by ancient belief systems, geology and dystopian visions, she has sought to evoke an otherworldliness through textiles. Using a combination of precious surfaces, engineered prints and sculptural forms, she transposes her dreams into wearable textile artworks.

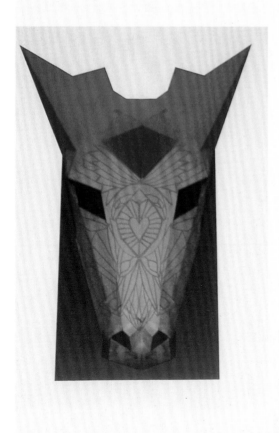

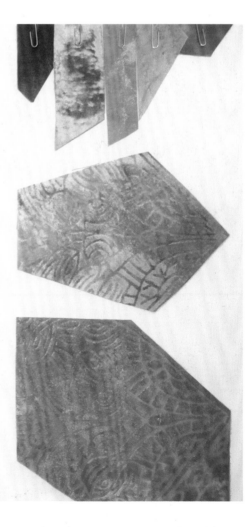

Senyor

Pablo

Senyor Pablo lives in Madrid, Spain, and makes knitwear. After working in advertising, the film industry and broadcasting production, costume design and at Atrezzo, he decided to change his career path and work in pre-technology.

He has made three collections of knitwear using a knitting machine. They combined graphic prints and were shown in Ego's showroom during Mercedes-Benz Fashion Week in Madrid.

Pablo has made knitwear for other designers such as Carlos Díez Díez and Krizia Robustella. He has also taken part in the project 'Eastpak Artist Studio' and at the international festival 'BYOB' (Bring Your Own Beamer) in Matadero, Madrid.

He promises to continue knitting to make winters nice, warm and friendly!

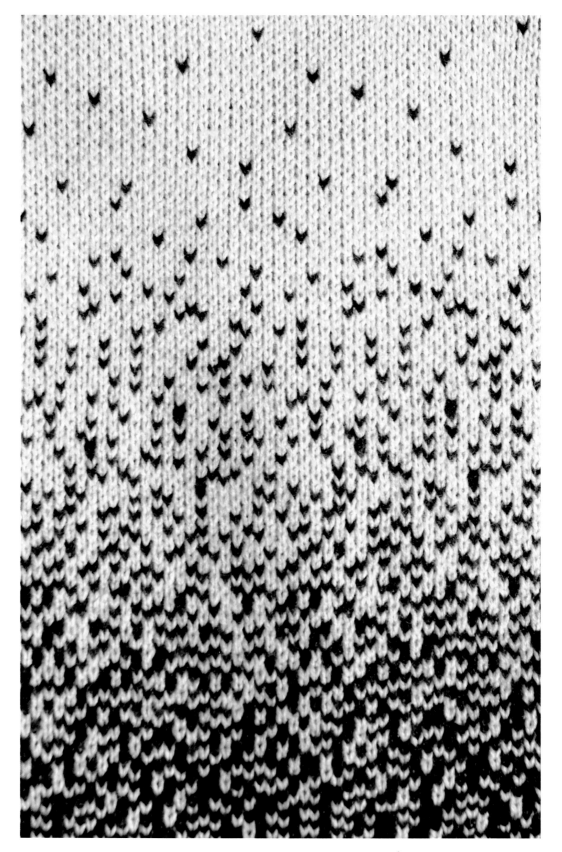

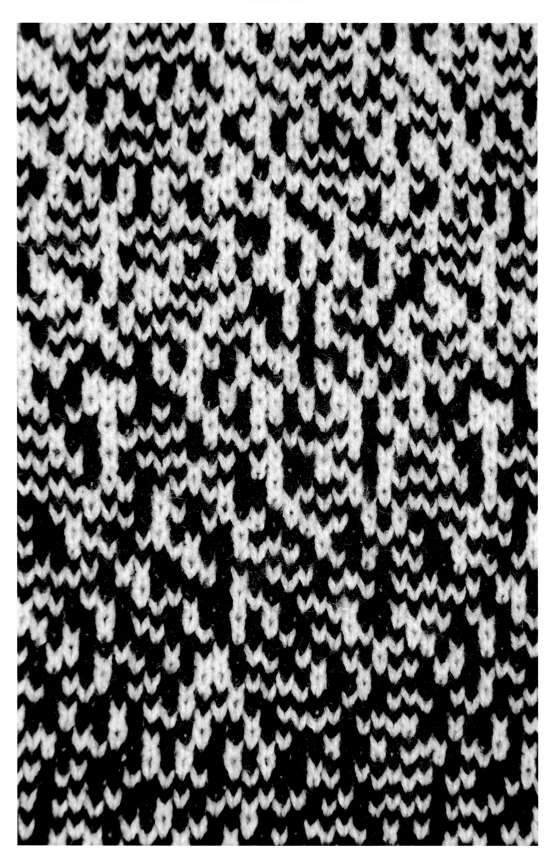

Dan
Riley &
Jeannine
Han

Dan Riley & Jeannine Han currently reside in New York City. Their engrossing projects have involved patterns and textiles, costumes, sound, sound as sculptures, performance, installations, paintings and technology.

Their experimental work finds new ways to use technology and visual axioms for performances and sound arts in site-specific environments. The correlation between sound and patterns is an integral part of their work and they aim to create art that is playful, yet intelligent, and excites greater cognitive levels in the viewer and the creators.

Riley and Han's work has become a catalyst in the realization and prognostication of a cycle of the world as we know it and fills the gaps between now and forever.

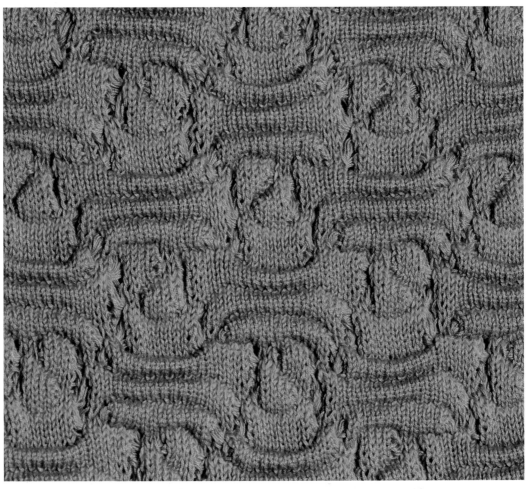

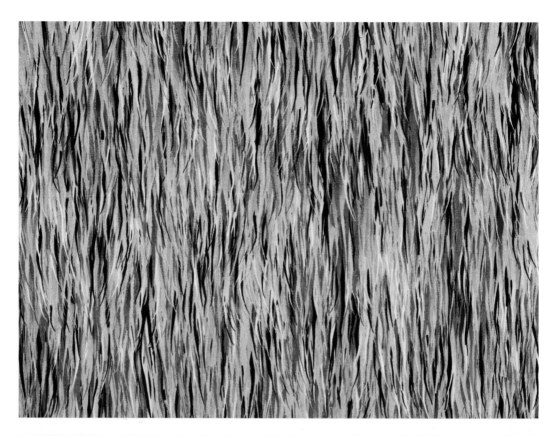

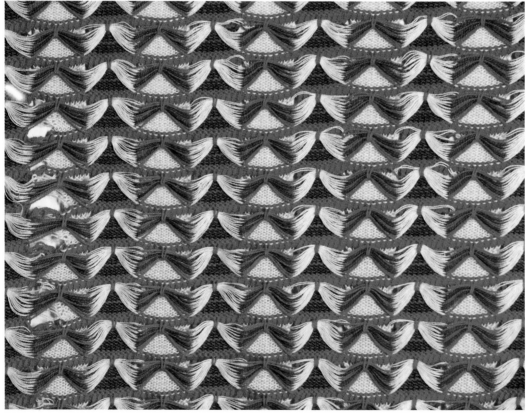

Kayla
Mattes

Kayla Mattes is a textile-based artist currently living in Los Angeles. She finished her Bachelor of Fine Arts in Textiles at Rhode Island School of Design in 2011.

Her work has been featured in *WAD* and *I Want You* magazines, and online on The Cool Hour, Make Space, Ecrans and The Creators Project. She has collaborated with Art is Shit Editions, the Los Angeles-based printshop and gallery, and recently finished designing a collection of printed tapestries for Urban Outfitters.

Mattes's jewelry line was launched with the Spring/Summer 2013 SUMMER CAMP collection. The collection both manipulated and paid homage to the lanyard braiding phenomenon, resulting in a collection of contemporary and unconventional geometric necklaces. The pieces are constructed entirely of machine-knit cords and hand 'gimped' plastic lace. Her work tends to comment on the nostalgia felt towards pop culture of the past and the influence of kitsch aesthetics on the development of 'high' art and culture.

Sabine **Ducasse**

Sabine Ducasse has lived in Shanghai, China, for more than four years, but she is originally from Paris. She was formerly a pediatric hematology nurse, but made a career change when she left for China and decided to attend a fashion design school in Shanghai. She was there from 2009 until 2012.

Ducasse's first collection, 'Melting Pot', was her graduation collection. It represents the fusion between her east meets west experience.

All the visions she has from east to west merge together to combine and create a new identity. The melted, seamless plastic pieces and the psychedelic, kaleidoscopic patterns represent the visions she has from the merging of east and west, and the idea of rebirth. They form her idea of 'a melting pot salad bowl' that she experiences every day as a foreigner in China.

Anna-Marie **Leppisaari**

Anna-Mari Leppisaari was born in 1986 in Finland and graduated in 2011 with a BA in Fashion Design from Aalto University in Helsinki, Finland. She studied textile design as part of her degree and her love of textures, patterns and structures can be seen in her work. She likes to experiment with techniques and combine traditional craftsmanship and new technology. This creates unexpected, but exquisite surfaces with fresh textures and playful patterns; the textiles are mixed with contemporary shapes to create elegant, but graphic and exciting looks.

Leppisaari was awarded the BMW prize at the Aalto University annual fashion show for her BA graduate collection in 2011. In August that year she was also the first runner up in Designers' Nest, a competition in Copenhagen, Denmark.

In the autumn of 2011 she started her MA studies at Aalto University and participated in the European textile trainee programme at Audax Textile Museum in Tilburg, the Netherlands, and later in Como, Italy. In Como, she worked as a print designer and in Audax, she designed and produced her own textiles, which formed the basis of her Spring/Summer 2013 collection inspired by contradictions and contrasts. She researched 3-D geometrics, tacky and inappropriate fashions, elegant and formal styles of dressing, and elements from couture and sportswear.

The collection was awarded the *A* magazine, Marimekko and *SSAW* magazine jury prize at Aalto University's annual fashion show in 2012. Dan Thawley, editor-in-chief of *A* magazine, said she was given the award for 'the breadth of creative and commercial vision, coupled with an extensive experimentation with unique woven fabrics, contemporary shapes and a fresh use of colour.' In August 2012, she showcased her Spring/Summer 2013 collection at Vision fair in Copenhagen.

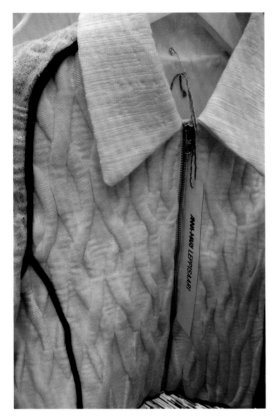

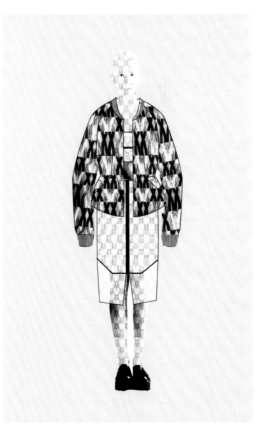

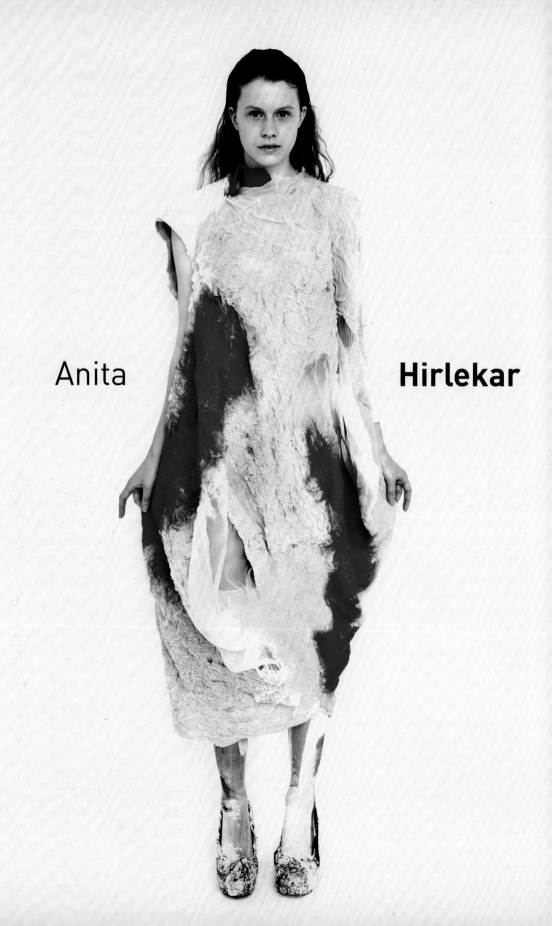

Anita Hirlekar

Anita Hirlekar is an Icelandic womenswear and textile designer based in London. She studied for a BA in Fashion Design with Print at Central Saint Martins in London and graduated in 2012.

Hirlekar's work consists of experiments with shape, colour and texture. She draws on her love of handmade goods and creates innovative fabric techniques, with traditional craftsmanship as her guide. Inspired by various abstract painters from Rothko to Richter, Hirlekar's starting point for her designs is thoughtful and artistic play with paint and colour. She merges dissimilar textures and diverse materials to create considered and unique clothing, reminiscent of a painting.

For her BA graduation collection Hirlekar focused on hand felting – she felts Merino wool on silk, knit, velvet, lace and polyester to achieve different textures and volumes. She also used this technique in the construction of the garments by felting large pieces of the cloth together, so that seams were not needed in the collection.

Hirlekar's work has been shown in Palos Verdes Art Center in Los Angeles, as well as the Museum of Design and Applied Art in Reykjavik. She has worked with Christian Dior Couture in Paris and Diane von Fürstenberg in New York. She is studying for an MA in Fashion Textiles at Central Saint Martins, London.

Jonah **Jacobs**

Jonah Jacobs is a Cleveland Area artist. He was born in Denmark, but has lived in the United States for most of his life. He graduated from Antioch College in Ohio and served in the army in South Korea and in the 82nd Airborne Division.

His goal as an artist is to educate people about the aesthetic possibilities of recycled materials. To achieve this, he incorporates everyday household objects, found objects and waste materials into his art. These materials are altered with paint, dyes, oils and other products. They are then combined into intricate and ornate pieces that resemble organic structures. By doing so, he hopes not only to introduce people to a new aesthetic possibility, but also to highlight some of the fundamental processes involved in nature.

It is not his intention to create works of art that are exact representations of organic structures – rather, his goal is to form unconventional materials into simple shapes such as a cone, a tube, or a sphere, and then use those simple shapes in repeated patterns to form complex structures.

The questions that Jacobs seeks to answer are: what is the role of repetition in establishing order and beauty in an organic structure? What types of structures can be made using waste materials and what are the aesthetic and physical imitations of those materials? How much of

a role does nature play versus the artist in the final composition of any given art piece?

Jacobs's artwork grapples with aesthetic ideas and explores some of the fundamental principles of nature.

Adrià

Colorado

Adrià Colorado's unmistakable marks are bold and innovative combinations of fabrics and prints.

Handmade and refined digital prints represent the DNA of the 24-year-old Catalan designer, who graduated from IDEP Barcelona. His designs are governed by comfort, originality and diversity.

Although this young designer has only emerged in the world of fashion in the last few years, his men's collection 'Le Maroc' was presented in Ego's showroom during Mercedes-Benz Fashion Week in Madrid in 2012. No one was indifferent to it. He also worked as part of a team for two collections with Martin Lamothe.

Colorado combines fashion design with a street avant-garde look, resulting in an expression of youth, joy, confidence and personality.

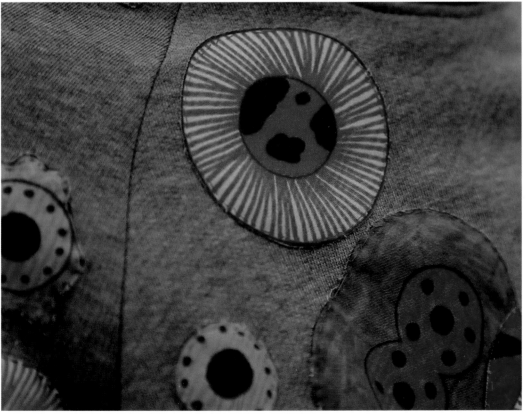

String **Theory**

String Theory is a partnership between two textile designers, one of whom specializes in knitting and the other in weaving.

String Theory's scarves and shawls are made from fabrics that are designed and produced in low runs with the help of small North American mills.

String Theory scarves and shawls are distinguished by their exclusive pattern designs and by the look and feel of their long-wearing quality. Knitted and woven with yarns such as Peruvian baby alpaca and Italian Merino, these fabrics are a pleasure to live in.

As constructed textile designers, String Theory work with the maths and physics of fibres, yarns, knitting and weaving to develop structure, pattern and texture. Consequently, they are inspired by structures and patterns observed in the built and natural world. Essentially, they are interested in how our world comes together and falls apart and the patterns that occur in the process.

The name String Theory is borrowed from a theory of physics that says the world is made of vibrating strings.

Meghan Price is an artist and woven textile designer. She was born in Montreal and is based in Toronto. Her career encompasses an active art practice, commissioned and collaborative design projects, and she teaches at the Ontario College of Art & Design University in Toronto. Price has a degree in Textile Construction from the Montreal Centre for Contemporary Textiles and a Master of Fine Arts with a specialization in Fibre from Concordia University in Montreal.

Lysanne Latulippe lives and works in Montreal. She has taught at the Montreal Centre for Contemporary Textiles since 2005. In 2000, she earned a diploma in Textile Construction. An expert in the field of knit design, she also consults and collaborates with businesses and independent fashion designers.

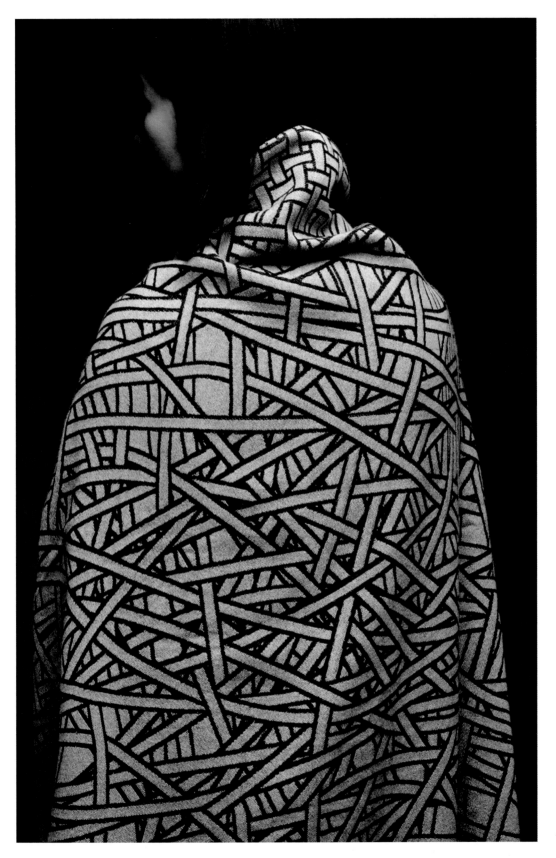

Abby
Thomas

Abby Thomas began her studies at the School of the Art Institute of Chicago in 2007. She first focused on fibre and material studies and then moved onto fashion design and construction. She graduated in 2012.

Her latest collection entitled 'June' (after her late maternal grandmother) is about savouring a heritage. Born and raised in a small town in North Carolina, Thomas rooted her concept in a collective Southern history. Unusually within the fashion industry, she chose to work with both menswear and womenswear. She created a synthesis between the two genres, 'They play upon each other, feed off one another in a certain way. I want people to notice that, embrace it, and use it to their advantage.'

The collection began to take form as Thomas collapsed the boundaries between her own, her mother's and her grandparents' histories. She blended the comforts, traditions and manners into silhouettes that both defy and embrace Southern gentility and traditions. 'It's a pride that is engrained in your being. It's who you are. It's who taught you how to be who you are. It's who you want to be. I come from a place often misunderstood, but when I leave it, it's all I can do to not pine away for it.'

Although the collection alludes to the South's troubled past of decadence and decay, it is balanced by a highly personal foundation. Looking through old family photographs sparked sun-bleached, tobacco-stained memories. The colour theme was inspired in part by 1960s dye-transfer prints of Southern photographer William Eggleston.

Thomas's collection is classic in silhouette but contemporary in its mix of colour, cut and materials. Sheer vintage flocked floral silk connects the present with the past in the form of wide-leg pants and a baby-doll top. Chambray jumpsuits for both genders remind us of the hard-working middle class. Clusters of vintage and costume jewels accompany a debutante gown that is corseted to show a young woman's figure. With an attached silk chiffon coverlet and ankle-length brocade, there is a suggestion of a gaudy old-moneyed world of plantations, excess and an innocence of Sunday best. Tobacco brown and peach linen cotton-blend suits are cut from Thomas's own cotton blossom print design and produced by North Carolina based company Spoonflower.

Thomas is currently exploring her career options in New York City and Los Angeles.

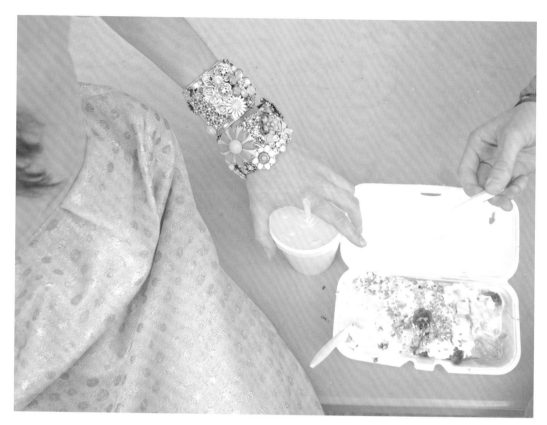

Designer Directory

ABBY THOMAS
www.abby-thomas.com
susanabigailthomas@gmail.com

**ADRIÀ COLORADO
BY ADRIAN FERNANDEZ
GRANADO**
www.adriacolorado.blogspot.com
adriacolorado@gmail.com

ALLURE DESIGNS
alluredesigns@outlook.com

ALYSE CZACK
www.alyseczack.com
alyseczack@gmail.com

AMANDA MCCAVOUR
www.amandamccavour.com

AMY JO LEWIS
www.amyjolewis.co.uk

ANDREA C. PURCELL
purcell.andreac@gmail.com

ANDREW WILLIAM ERDRICH
www.bigurges.com
andrewerdrich@gmail.com

ANGE YAKE
www.angeyake.com
ange@angeyake.com

ANITA HIRLEKAR
anita.hirlekar@gmail.com

ANNA OGUIENKO
www.annaoguienko.com
hello@annaoguienko.com

ANNA-MARI LEPPISAARI
www.annamarileppisaari.com
annamari.leppisaari@gmail.com

ANNELINE SOPHIA
www.annelinesophiadesigns.com
info@annelinesophiadesigns.com

**APRIL NOGA
PRILLAMENA**
www.aprilnoga.com
aprilnoga@gmail.com

**AUDREY VICTORIA KEIFFER
THE PATTERNBASE**
www.audreyvictoriakeiffer.com
audrey.keiffer@gmail.com

BABI BRASILEIRO
www.babibrasileiro.com
contacto@babibrasileiro.com

BEBEL FRANCO
www.bebelfranco.com.br
bebelfranco@bebelfranco.com.br

BECKABONCE
www.beckabonce.co.uk
rw.beckabonce@hotmail.co.uk

BECKY HODGSON
beckylouisehodgson@gmail.com

BETHAN JANINE
www.bethanjaninedesigns.tumblr.com
bethanjanine@gmail.com

BETS KUMOR
www.reposeinteriors.net
elizabeth@reposeinteriors.net

**BRENDA SUTTON
BREN MICHELLE DESIGN**
www.brenmichelledesign.co.nz

**BRITT + LEIGH
BY BRITTNEY LEIGHANN**
www.brittandleigh.com
brittandleigh@gmail.com

CANTOINETTE STUDIOS
www.cantoinettestudios.com
cantoinettestudios@gmail.com

CASEY MOLLETT
www.casey-mollett.co.uk
cmollett91@gmail.com

CHARLOTTE LINTON
www.charlottelinton.com
info@charlottelinton.com

CHARLOTTE MASON
www.charlottemasondesign.co.uk
charlottemasondesign@gmail.com

CHELSEA DENSMORE
www.chelsdens.wix.com/textiledesign

CIARAH COENEN
www.cargocollective.com/ciarahcoenen
ciarahcoenen@gmail.com

CJ HUNGERMAN
www.bluecanvas.com/randomrobot
rrastudio24@yahoo.com

CLAIRE BROWN
www.society6.com/
clairebrownsurfacepattern
claireradcliff@btinternet.com

CLAIRE BUCKLEY
www.behance.net/clairebuckley
clairebuck18@hotmail.com

CLAIRE LEGGETT
www.claireleggett.co.uk
hello@claireleggett.co.uk

CLARE VICKERY
www.clarevickery.com
info@clarevickery.com

CONNIE UTTERBACK
cutterback@earthlink.net

DAN RILEY & JEANNINE HAN
www.scisci.org
info@scisci.org

DANIELA GUARIN
www.danielaguarin.com
dguarin92@gmail.com

DAWN CLARKSON
www.dawnclarkson.com

DELLA REAMS
www.dellareams.com
dellareams@gmail.com

DEMI-GOUTTE
www.demigoutte.blogspot.fr
v.ozanon@gmail.com

DIANA PALERMO
www.dianapalermo.com
poste@gmail.com

DUSTIN WILLIAMS
www.sorrysorrytown.com
sorrysorrytown@gmail.com

**ELI ARIZTEGIETA
RIZTYDESIGN**
www.riztydesign.wordpress.com
riztydesign@gmail.com

ELIN NOBLE
www.elinnoble.com
elin@ElinNoble.com

ELLE LEHMANN
www.foxesdoingthetango.tumblr.com

EMILY JEANNE OTT
emily.jeanne.ott@gmail.com

EMMA BURROW DESIGN
www.emmaburrow.co.uk
studio@emmaburrow.co.uk

EMMA COPE
www.emmacopedesign.tumblr.com
emmacope01@hotmail.co.uk

EMMA FORMSTONE
www.emmaformstone.blogspot.com

**ERIN WOOTTEN
erinandmarie**
www.erinwootten.com
em@erinwootten.com

ETTA SANDRY
etta.sandry@gmail.com

FAYE BROWN DESIGNS
www.fayebrowndesigns.com
hello@fayebrowndesigns.com

FEMI FORD ART & DESIGN
www.femiford.com
info@femiford.com

FIONA STOLTZE
www.fionastoltze.com
fionastoltz@gmail.com

GABRIELA LARIOS
www.gabrielalarios.com
creativestudio@gabrielalarios.com

GARRY NOLAND
www.garrynolandart.com/home.html
garrynoland@gmail.com

GRACE MICHIKO HAMANN
www.grace-hamann.squarespace.com
gracie.michiko@gmail.com

GWYNED TREFETHEN
www.gwynedtrefethen.com
gwynedtrefethen@mac.com

HANDMADE BY SARA CRAMER
www.miss-cramer.com
handmadebysaracramer@gmail.com

HANNAH THAYER JOHNSON
www.variablequilt.tumblr.com

HANNAH TRURAN
www.hannahtruran.co.uk
info@hannahtruran.co.uk

H. SCOTT ROTH
www.hscottroth.com
hscottroth@gmail.com

HERBERT LOUREIRO
www.cargocollective.com/herbert-loureiro
herbbbert@gmail.com

IAN ADDISON HALL
www.dontnotlook.com

INGRID JOHNSON
www.ingridjo.com
spoonknifefork@gmail.com

ISABEL LUCENA
www.isabellucena.com

**JACQUELINE AUVIGNE
FINE ART & PATTERN**
www.jacquelineauvigne.com
jacqueline.auvigne@gmail.com

JANE OGREN
www.janeogren.com

JANNA ROKÜSEK
www.cargocollective.com/
jannarokusek
jcrokusek@gmail.com

JAQUELINA FREITAS
www.jaquelinafreitas.tumblr.com
jaquelinafreitas@gmail.com

JASMIN ELISA GUERRERO
jasmin.elisa.guerrero@gmail.com

**JEFFREY ISOM
PRE SENSE FORM**
www.presenseform.com

JELENA DIMITRIJEVIC
www.jelenadimitrijevic.com

JEN GIN
www.jen-gin.com
gin.jennifer@gmail.com

JENNIE WHITHAM
JLW ILLUSTRATION
www.jlwillustration.com
jennie_whitham@yahoo.co.uk

JENNIFER D'EUGENIO
www.cargocollective.com/
deugeniodesigns
jenn@deugeniodesigns.com

JESSIE MACAW
A SIDE PROJECT
www.asideproject.co.nz
jessie@nineteena.co.nz

JOLENE HECKMAN
JOLENE INK
www.joleneheckman.blogspot.com
jogr4@yahoo.com

JONAH JACOBS
www.jonahjacobs.com
bosse_de_nage73@yahoo.com

JOY O. UDE
www.joyoftextiles.com
joyoftextiles@gmail.com

JUSTINE ALDERSEY-WILLIAMS
www.justinealderseywilliams.com

KATHRYN PLEDGER
www.kathrynpledger.com
pledger@gmail.com

KATY CLEMMANS
SURFACE PATTERN DESIGN
www.katyclemmans.co.uk
hello@katyclemmans.co.uk

KAYLA MATTES
www.kaylamattes.com
contact@kaylamattes.com

KELLY PARSELL
www.kellyparsell.com

KRISTA JO MUSTAIN
www.kristajomustain.tumblr.com
kristajmustain@gmail.com

KRISTEN PICKELL
WOVEN NOSTALGIA
kristenpickell@gmail.com

KRISTI O'MEARA
THE PATTERNBASE
www.kristiomeara.com
www.thepatternbase.com
thepatternbase@gmail.com

LAUREN ELIZABETH KRISCHER
www.lekrischer.blogspot.com

LESLEY MEROLA MOYA
HUNT + GATHER STUDIO
www.huntandgatherstudio.com
info@huntandgatherstudio.com

LEXIE STOIA
www.lexiestoia.com
info@lexiestoia.com

LIZ SMITH
ELLE JANE DESIGNS
www.ellejanedesigns.com
mail@ellejanedesigns.com

LIZ WEISSERT
www.lizweissert.com

LORENZO NANNI
www.lorenzonanni.com
lorenzonanni@gmail.com

LOUISE MILLS TEXTILES
www.louisemillstextiles.wordpress.com
louisesherry2@hotmail.co.uk

LUCY HARDCASTLE
www.lucyhardcastle.com
lucyhardcastle@live.co.uk

LYNNETTE MIRANDA
www.lynnettemiranda.com
lynnettemiranda@gmail.com

MARAYA RODOSTIANOS
PRINT PAPER CLOTH
www.printpapercloth.com
info@printpapercloth.com

MARCIA L. WEISS
weissm@philau.edu

MARGHERITA PORRA
ARITHMETIC CREATIVE
www.arithmeticcreative.com
m@arithmeticcreative.com

MARIA JOSÉ BAUTISTA V
MAJOBV
www.majobv.com
info@majobv.com

MARIE DELISLE HOLMBERG
CHICKAPRINT
www.chickaprint.com
mariedh@hotmail.co.uk

MARIE-THERESE WISNIOWSKI
ART QUILL STUDIO
www.artquill.blogspot.com.au
studio@artquill.com.au

MARTA SPENDOWSKA
www.martaspendowska.com
contact@martaspendowska.com

MARTIN LEON
MALE ®
www.guaizine.com
jmld2@hotmail.com

MEL SMITH DESIGNS
www.melsmithdesigns.com
mail@melsmithdesigns.com

MICHAEL EARL
www.michaelearl.net
mail@michaelearl.net

MICHELE CASTELLANO
www.michelecastellano.com
michele@michelecastellano.com

MICHELLE MANOLOV
PATTERN AND CO
www.patternandco.com
contact@patternandco.com

MIRANDA MOL
www.mirandamol.com
info@mirandamol.com

NAOMI HEFETZ
naomihefetz@yahoo.co.uk

NATALIE ALEXANDER
www.nataliealex.com
natalie@nataliealex.com

NATALIE K. DAVIES
nataliekdavies@hotmail.co.uk

NATASHA BUGG
www.natashabugg.tumblr.com
natashabugg@live.co.uk

NELDA WARKENTIN
www.neldawarkentin.com

OLIVIA MEW
www.oliviamew.com
hi@oliviamew.com

ONNEKE
www.onneke.com
onnekevw@gmail.com

PATRICK MORRISSEY
www.pat-morrissey.com
morrisseypatrick7@gmail.com

POONAM DHUFFER
MAHA DHUFFER
www.dhuffer.tumblr.com
www.maha-dhuffer.tumblr.com
pdhuffer@gmail.com

RACHEL GRESHAM DESIGN
www.rachelgreshamdesign.com
oneplumspot@gmail.com

ROSHANNAH BAGLEY
www.behance.net/roshannahbagley
roshannahbagley@gmail.com

SABERAH MALIK
www.saberahmalik.com
hmsaberah@yahoo.com

SAM JAFFE
www.samjaffe.org

SANDEE HJORTH
www.sandeehjorth.com

SARAH ENGLISH
PATTERN STATE
www.patternstate.com

SARAH WOTHERS
www.sarahwothers.com

SCHATZI BROWN
BY TANYA BROWN
www.schatzibrown.com
schatzibrown@gmail.com

SCHAULEH VIVIAN SAHBA
BOUCLÉ, SF
www.bouclesf.com
sho@bouclesf.com

SENYOR PABLO
www.senyorpablo.com
info@senyorpablo.com

SIAN ELIN
www.sianelin.com
info@sianelin.com

SIMI GAUBA
www.simidesign.com
simi@simidesign.com

SOPHIE COLLOM
www.sophiecollom.com

SOPHIE THOMPSON
www.sophiethompsondesign.tumblr.com
sophie.thompson@rocketmail.com

STRING THEORY
www.stringtheory.ws
info@stringtheory.ws

SUSAN JOHNSON
AVALANCHE LOOMS
www.avalancheLooms.com
susan@avalancheLooms.com

TALI FURMAN
tali.furman@network.rca.ac.uk

TAYLOR TELYAN
www.taylortelyan.com
taylortelyan@gmail.com

TINA OLSSON
FYLLAYTA
www.fyllayta.wordpress.com
tina.olsson.design@gmail.com

URSULA SMITH
www.easyscraps.com
ursula@easyscraps.com

VANESSA HAFEZI
www.vanessahafezi.com
vhafezi@hotmail.com

VERONICA GALBRAITH
www.verogalbraith.co.uk
talktome@verogalbraith.co.uk

VICTORIA MARTINEZ
www.victoria-martinez.com
victoriamartinez21st@gmail.com

VICTORIA SNAPE
www.victoriasnape.co.uk
vicsdesign@yahoo.co.uk

YOUNG CHO
www.young-cho.com
youngcho815@gmail.com

ZIA GIPSON
ART ISLE STUDIOS
www.ziagipson.com
zia@whidbey.net

ZOE ATTWELL
www.zoeattwell.com
zoe@zoeattwell.com

Photo Credits

The author and publisher would like to thank all the artists featured in this book, as well as the following individuals for providing photographic images. Every effort has been made to trace the copyright holders. We apologize in advance for any unintentional omissions and would be pleased to insert the appropriate acknowledgments in any subsequent edition of this publication.

pp. 41, 245 [centre left + right], 255 [above left] **Harrison Telyan**
p. 61 [centre right] **Robert Chase Heishman**
p. 163 **Photographed and edited by Poonam Dhuffer**
pp. 203 [centre left], 260, **Tariq Malik MD**
pp. 236, 237 [bottom], 239 [above left] **Graeme Mills**
pp. 238, 250, 251 **Etta Sandry**
pp. 239 [below], 253 [below] **Photography by Hannah Sutherland**
pp. 239 [above right], 245 [bottom], 302, 303 [below], 304, 306 **Henrik Bengtsson**
pp. 241, 243 [bottom left + right] **Della Reams**
p. 249 **Chesley Williams**
p. 252 **John Tuckey**
p. 253 [above] **Photography by Moomin Kheir**
p. 257 [above right] **David Caras**
pp. 258, 259 [below right] **Garry Noland**
p. 262 **Neil Alexander**
p. 267 **Produced with the support of the Ontario Arts Council**
pp. 268, 269 **Sara Cramer**
pp. 274, 275 [above], 276, 278, 279 **Lorenzo Nanni**
pp. 275 [below], 277 **Alexandre Dieval**
pp. 280, 283, 284 **Mark Champion**
pp. 286, 288, 290, 292 **Direction and editing: Hannah Truran. Photographer: Dominic Tscudin. Model: Skye Victoria. Make up: Bethany Swan**
pp. 287, 289, 291 [above], 285 **Hannah Truran**
p. 291 **Dominic Tschudin**
pp. 294, 295 [below left], 296, 299, 300 **Photographer: Javier Morán. Model: Roberto Martínez**
p. 295 [above right] **Matías Uris**
p. 305 **Photographer: Henrik Bengtsson. Model: Faseeh Saleem**
p. 307 **Photographer: Henrik Bengtsson. Model: Abril Vergara Lozano**
p. 308 **Andre Herrero**
pp. 310–15 **IN RESIDENCE**
pp. 316–21, 321 **Photographer: Matthias Hossann. Model: Ding Rouying**
p. 317 [below] **Photographer: Matthias Hossann**
pp. 322, 324, 325 **Sofia Okkonen**
pp. 323 [above], 328, 329 [above right, below left + below right] **Anna-Mari Leppisaari**
pp. 326, 327 [below] **Matilda Nieminen**
pp. 330, 331 [above], 334–35, 337–39 **Saga Sig**
pp. 331 [below], 333, 336 **Anita Hirlekar**
pp. 346–51 **Josep Prat Sorolla**
pp. 352–57 **Frederic Bouchard**
pp. 358–63 **All garments and jewelry by Abby Thomas. All photos courtesy of Caleb Condit**

Index

A Very Heartfelt Thanks to our Kickstarter Donors

From the bottom of my heart, I would like to thank everyone who contributed to our book project. Your donations and support mean so much to me, and have made it possible to release a wonderful resource to the public and the design community! Thank you for believing in this project and making this dream come true! I couldn't have made it happen without you!

Sincerely,

Kristi O'Meara

// Andrew Cimelli
// Andy Montee
// April Camlin
// Audrey Victoria Keiffer
// Barbara Wright
// Becky Hodgson
// Bethania Lima
// Bets Kumor
// Brandon Eaker
// Bread Boys!
// Brian Paul Rowan
// Caroline Killhour (Hui No'eau)
// Cathy Hsiao & Kids in Love Collective
// David White
// Dustin Brown
// Ellen Wersan
// Emma Burrow
// Emma Cope
// Etta Sandry
// Femi Ford

// Garry Noland
// Haley Martin
// Jason Judd
// Jeanne White
// Jen Grygiel
// Jerry O'Meara
// Joseph Taylor Mcrae
// Joy O. Ude
// Katherina London
// Kathy Cho
// Kathy O'Meara
// Kayla Mattes
// Kelly Parsell
// Lori Mattes
// Luis Rodriguez
// Lynnette Miranda
// Marci Villa
// Mark Cason
// Mary Beth Yates
// Meghan McLauren
// Michael B. Payne
// Michael Earl

// Neelybat Chestnut
// Nicole He
// Nicoshene Simpson
// Nina Chidich
// Olivia Mew
// Rebecca Brown
// Rita Minissi
// Ryan Riley
// Sara Cramer
// Sarah Moore
// Schauleh Vivian Sahba
// Silas Reeves
// Sneaky Creeps
// Steven B. Wheeler
// Susan Furr
// Thorne Brandt
// Tim Sandry
// Trevor Powers
// Vanessa Hafezi
// Victor Ude
// Whitney Lorene Wood
// Wyatt Grant